"[Ram] Dass delves into th[...] fy most of us—and affirms there is an awareness in each of us that transcends all the attributes that necessarily diminish with age. Ram Dass shows readers of all ages that it is possible to stay present in the midst of suffering, to be still and know that God is here now."
—*Publishers Weekly*

"Ram Dass is a superb writer. His example of gentleness and loving compassion is infused with profound wisdom of the heart and mind, a welcome sense of humor and a savvy effectiveness in the real world." —*San Francisco Chronicle*

"This book is an astonishing gift of love and clarity. Ram Dass guides us through many dimensions of aging with courage, humor, and profound wisdom." —Sharon Salzberg, author of *Lovingkindness* and *A Heart as Wide as the World*

"Ram Dass has entered the often stormy relationship between our physical and spiritual sides, and he has lived to tell about it. This is no gussied up, glossed over personal account of illness, but an honest, courageous book that flows from the soul. Listen up, everybody, while Ram Dass tells it like it is." —Larry Dossey, M.D., author of *Reinventing Medicine* and *Healing Words*

continued . . .

ALSO BY RAM DASS *(Richard Alpert)*

IDENTIFICATION AND CHILD REARING

THE PSYCHEDELIC EXPERIENCE

LSD

BE HERE NOW

GRIST FOR THE MILL

JOURNEY OF AWAKENING

MIRACLE OF LOVE

HOW CAN I HELP?

COMPASSION IN ACTION

RAM DASS

Edited by
MARK MATOUSEK AND MARLENE ROEDER

RIVERHEAD BOOKS
New York

STILL HERE

Embracing Aging, Changing, and Dying

RIVERHEAD BOOKS
Published by the Penguin Group
Penguin Group (USA) Inc.
375 Hudson Street, New York, New York 10014, USA
Penguin Group (Canada), 90 Eglinton Avenue East, Suite 700, Toronto, Ontario M4P 2Y3, Canada
(a division of Pearson Penguin Canada Inc.) • Penguin Books Ltd., 80 Strand, London WC2R 0RL,
England • Penguin Group Ireland, 25 St. Stephen's Green, Dublin 2, Ireland (a division of Penguin
Books Ltd.) • Penguin Group (Australia), 250 Camberwell Road, Camberwell, Victoria 3124, Australia
(a division of Pearson Australia Group Pty. Ltd.) • Penguin Books India Pvt. Ltd., 11 Community
Centre, Panchsheel Park, New Delhi—110 017, India • Penguin Group (NZ), 67 Apollo Drive,
Rosedale, Auckland 0632, New Zealand (a division of Pearson New Zealand Ltd.) • Penguin Books
(South Africa) (Pty.) Ltd., 24 Sturdee Avenue, Rosebank, Johannesburg 2196, South Africa

Penguin Books Ltd., Registered Offices: 80 Strand, London WC2R 0RL, England

Permissions and credits can be found on p. 207.

Copyright © 2000 by Ram Dass
Book design by Deborah Kerner
Cover design © Walter Harper
Photograph of the author © Lisa Law

First Riverhead hardcover edition: May 2000
First Riverhead trade paperback edition: June 2001
Riverhead trade paperback ISBN: 978-1-57322-871-8

The Library of Congress has catalogued the Riverhead hardcover edition as follows:

Ram Dass.
Still here : embracing aging, changing, and dying / Ram Dass.
p. cm.
ISBN 1-57322-049-3
1. Aged. 2. Aging. 3. Aging—Psychological aspects. 4. Aging—Religious aspects. 5. Ageism.
HQ1061.R285   2000   99-086015
305.26—dc21

PRINTED IN THE UNITED STATES OF AMERICA

To Neem Karoli Baba

ACKNOWLEDGMENTS

There are so many people to thank. First, I would like to thank Tara Bennett Goleman for enticing me into teaching our first conscious aging course together many years ago. There were also a number of fellow faculty at the Omega seminar for Conscious Aging Conference in 1992 whom I would also like to thank: Rabbi Zalman Schachter, Drew Leder, Bob Atchley, Connie Goldman, Rick Moody, Tom Cole, Carter Williams, and Carol Segrave.

I would also like to thank the members of the "aging class" in Marin.

Thank you to my father and the other older people I've met along the way. Thank you to the people whose deaths I have been present for.

And to Dan Goleman, Roger Walsh, Frances Vaughn, and Stephen and Ondrea Levine, for their metaphysical guidance.

Thank you to my superb editor, Amy Hertz, and my publisher, Susan Petersen Kennedy. They taught me how compassionate a publisher can be.

Thank you to Jai Lakshman, for taking care of the nuts and bolts.

I would like to thank those people who helped me to find the words to finish this book after my stroke: Bokara Legendre, Shana Walter, Jo Anne Baughan, Mark Matousek, and Marlene Roeder.

CONTENTS

STILL HERE

PREFACE

Be Here Now was first published in 1971. It recorded the two major experiences I had had during the Sixties: one of them was psilocyben mushrooms, and the other was my guru, Maharajji. Both of them—mushrooms and Maharajji—did many things for me, one of which was to give me a familiarity with other planes of consciousness. They showed me that there's much more in any given moment than we usually perceive, and that we ourselves are much more than we usually perceive. When you know that, part of you can stand outside the drama of your life.

There were a number of transformations in Richard Alpert (my name at birth), which were inspired by mushrooms and Maharajji, and the best, I think, is the one that opened my heart and gave me a chance to serve. For me, the way the compassion seemed to express itself was through showing people what I had done, how I had approached my experiences, and so opening avenues for them where their own spirit could emerge. I felt incredibly fortunate because of all the things that had happened to me in the Sixties, and I wanted to spread the grace around. So there were lectures, there were books, there were tapes, and there were videos—a patchwork of different means for sharing my life with people. Gandhi once said, "My life is my message." That's what I aspire to.

As I opened my heart, various forms of suffering in my fellow human beings presented themselves, and I decided to do what I could to help. Prisoners read *Be Here Now*, and then wrote to me, and through corresponding with them I realized that many people can do deep spiritual work in prison. So I started the Prison Ashram Project.

Then I noticed how frightened we are of death in our culture, and what a lot of suffering that was creating. That was in contrast to what I'd seen in India, which has a much different understanding of death than we do because of their knowledge of the continuation of the soul. I wanted to find ways of sharing that, so I instituted the Dying Project. I started hanging out with people who were dying—including my mother, my father, my stepmother, people with AIDS and cancer, many, many people over the years, whom I've been with as they died. To each of these individuals and situations I brought what I had to share— my acquaintance with other planes of consciousness, and the way that affects how we perceive our living and our dying.

I started to look at the social institutions in the world around me, to see whether the spiritual tack I was taking might be commensurate with social action. A couple of friends were starting the Seva Foundation, and invited me to join them to work with doctors and activists, doing work in India, Nepal, and Guatemala, and with American Indians and in the inner cities of America. Other friends had wondered how business, which is the institution which has the most power in our society, might become more informed by spiritual Awareness and started the Social Venture Network. They are compassionate businesspeople who invited me to work together with them. I joined the board of Creating Our Future, which was an organization for teenagers who wanted to inform their lives with spirit. These organizations were trying to prevent suffering in areas in which I felt a personal connection. For some people, it's world hunger, or literacy. For me it was seeking spiritual answers to many of our problems.

My interest in aging came from a personal direction: I was getting older—and so were the baby boomers, who were fast approaching fifty. In this youth-oriented culture, aging is a profound source of suffering, and that is what I was responding to when I decided to turn my attention to conscious aging workshops, and to writing this book.

One evening in February 1997, I was in bed at home in Marin Country, contemplating how to end this book. I'd been working on the manuscript for the past eighteen months, weaving together material from personal experience and from talks I'd given around the country on conscious aging, but somehow the book's conclusion had eluded me. Lying there in the dark, I wondered why what I'd written seemed so incomplete, not quite rounded, grounded, or whole. I tried to imagine what life would be like if I were *very* old—not an active person of sixty-five, traveling the world incessantly as a teacher and speaker, caught up in my public role—but as someone of ninety, say, with failing sight and failing limbs. I fantasized how that old man would think, how he'd move and speak and hear, what desires he might have as he slowly surveyed the world. I was trying to *feel* my way into oldness. I was thoroughly enjoying this fantasy when the phone rang. In the process of my fantasy, I'd noticed that my leg seemed to have fallen asleep. As I got up to answer the phone, my leg gave way under me and I fell to the floor. In my mind, the fall was still part of my "old-man fantasy." I didn't realize that my leg was no longer working because I'd had a stroke.

I reached for my phone, on the table near my bed.

"R. D.? Are you there?"

I heard the voice of an old friend in Santa Fe. When I didn't respond coherently, he asked, "Are you sick?" I suppose I still didn't answer, so he said, "If you can't speak, tap on the phone.

Tap once for yes and twice for no." When he asked whether I wanted help, I tapped "no" over and over again.

Nonetheless, he contacted my secretaries, who live close by, and the next thing I knew they rushed into the house and found me on the floor. There I was flat on my back, still caught in my "dream" of the very old man, who had now fallen down because his leg wouldn't work. My assistants seemed very frightened; they called 911. My next recollection is of a group of young firemen, straight out of central casting, staring into the old man's face while I observed the whole thing as if from a doorway to the side. I'm told I was immediately rushed to a hospital nearby, but all I remember is being rolled down the hospital corridors, looking up at the ceiling pipes and the concerned faces of nurses and friends. I was fascinated by what was happening.

Only afterward did I learn that I had a stroke and realize how close to death I had actually been. The doctors told my friends I had a massive cerebral hemorrhage, and only a ten percent chance of survival. I noticed the looks of deep concern on the faces of the doctors and my friends, but the thought of dying was nowhere in my mind, so I was perplexed by their grave expressions.

Three hospitals and hundreds of hours of rehabilitation later, I gradually eased into my new post-stroke life as someone in a wheelchair, partially paralyzed, requiring round-the-clock care and a degree of personal attention that made me uncomfortable. All my life I had been a "helper"; I had even collaborated on a book called *How Can I Help?* I now found myself forced to accept the help of others, and to admit that my body needed attention. Because I'd spent my adult life concentrating on the realms of the spirit, I'd always been able to rationalize the distance I maintained from my body by saying that my detachment was a spiritual witnessing of the physical form. But that had been only partly true. The truth is that I distanced myself from my body. I saw my body as merely a vehicle for the soul. I ignored it as much as possible and tried to spiritualize it away.

From a physical perspective, the lack of love I'd shown toward my body contributed to my stroke. I was negligent about taking my blood pressure medicine and, a month before the stroke, ignored an unusual one-side hearing loss while scuba diving in the Caribbean. Before the stroke, although I was in my 60's, I saw myself as young and powerful, with my MG, golf clubs, surfing, and speaking gigs. Illness had shattered my self-image, and opened the door to a new chapter in my life.

After any major physical "insult," as they call it, it's all too easy to see yourself as a collection of symptoms rather than as a total human being, including your spirit—and thus to become your illness. Fear is powerful and contagious, and at first I allowed myself to catch it, worried that if I didn't do what the doctors ordered, I'd be sorry. But now I'm learning to take my healing into my own hands. Healing is not the same as curing, after all; healing does not mean going back to the way things were before, but rather allowing *what is now* to move us closer to God.

For example, since my speech was severely impaired by this stroke, I considered not speaking publicly anymore, since the words came so slowly, but people insisted that my halting new voice enabled them to concentrate on the silence between the words. Now that I speak more slowly, people tend to finish my sentences for me, and thus to answer questions for themselves. Though I once used silence as a teaching method, it now arises without my control and allows for a sense of emptiness, an emptiness that listeners can use as a doorway to their inner quiet.

My guru once said to a visitor complaining about her suffering, "I love suffering. It brings me so close to God." In this same way, I've learned that the incidents associated with aging—including this stroke—can be used for our spiritual healing, provided we learn to see through new eyes.

Although my outward life has been radically altered, I don't see myself as a stroke victim. I see myself as a Soul who's watching "him" experience the aftermath of this cerebral hemorrhage. Having accepted my predicament, I'm much happier than I was before. This troubles some of the people around me. They have told me that I should fight to walk again, but I don't know if I want to walk. I'm sitting—that's where I am. I'm peaceful like this and I am grateful to the people who care for me. Why is this wrong? Though I can now stand and move around with a walker, I've grown to love my wheelchair (I call it my swan boat) and being wheeled about by people who care. They carry Chinese emperors and Indian *maharajas* on palanquins; in other cultures, it's a symbol of honor and power to be carried and wheeled. I don't believe it's all-important to be what our culture calls "optimal."

Before the stroke I wrote a great deal about the terrible things that can happen in aging, and how to cope with them. Now I'm happy to say that having gone through what some would view as the worst, it's not so bad after all.

Getting old isn't easy for a lot of us. Neither is living, neither is dying. We struggle against the inevitable and we all suffer because of it. We have to find another way to look at the whole process of being born, growing old, changing, and dying, some kind of perspective that might allow us to deal with what we perceive as big obstacles without having to be dragged through the drama. It really helps to understand that we have something—that we *are* something—which is unchangeable, beautiful, completely aware, and continues no matter what. Knowing this doesn't solve everything—this is what I encountered and told about in *Be Here Now*, and I've still had my share of suffering. But the perspective of the soul can help a lot with the little things, and it is my hope that you'll be able to take from this book some joy in being "still here."

Recently, a friend said to me, "You're more human since the stroke than you were before." This touched me profoundly. What a gift the stroke has given me, to finally learn that I don't have to renounce my humanity in order to be spiritual—that I can be both witness and participant, both eternal spirit and aging body. The book's ending, which had eluded me, is now finally clear. The stroke has given me a new perspective to share about aging, a perspective that says, "Don't be a wise elder, be an incarnation of wisdom." That changes the whole nature of the game. That's not just a new role, it's a new state of being. It's the real thing. At nearly seventy, surrounded by people who care for and love me, I'm still learning to be here now.

1

SLIPPING
OUT OF
ZUMBACH'S
COAT

B irthdays were never traumatic for me, largely because I tried to ignore them. They came and went, I aged and forgot, and went along my merry way until I arrived at 60. That year, for the first time, I began to take notice of how old I was. In India, where I've spent a great deal of time, entering one's seventh decade is a defining moment, the threshold to a stage of life when we're meant to turn away from worldly things and focus attention on God. This seemed like a momentous passage, and during that birthday week I surrendered to three different parties, in three different parts of the country, each celebrating my coming of age.

For about six months, I tried "being" sixty, thinking of myself in that context. I wondered about how my life should change, who I should work toward becoming now that I was officially old. I thought about winding up my worldly affairs and, though most of my life had been devoted to spiritual matters, retreating even further from worldly temptations. But after a half-year, this notion began to seem like a bogus mind trip. Nothing had changed inside me; I didn't feel at all like sixty—or any age whatsoever—and as for giving up my outer activities, I was busier than ever. I decided to give up on being an old man and returned to the life I had before, forgetting that I was aging.

Two years later, at sixty-two, I had another wake-up call. On a soft autumn evening in 1993, I was on a train between Connecticut and New York admiring the brilliant New England foliage after a day spent hiking with a dear friend in the woodlands surrounding her home. I was deeply contented there on the coach, reflecting on the colors of the day, when a conductor came down the aisle, collecting tickets.

"I'll have to buy mine from you," I said.

"What kind will it be?" he asked.

"Do I have a choice?"

"Regular or senior citizen?"

Now, although I was bald, covered with age spots and battling high blood pressure and gout, it had never ever occurred to me—not once—that I could be called a senior citizen! I remembered the time when I was eighteen and tried to buy a beer legally in a bar, and was astounded that they'd sell one to *me*. But this conductor hadn't asked for ID; he'd taken one look and thought, "Discount." Offended, amused, confused, I said in a squeaky-sounding voice, "Senior citizen?"

"That'll be four and a half dollars," he said.

"How much would the regular ticket be?"

"Seven dollars."

Well, I was pleased with that, of course, but the satisfaction of saving the money quickly faded. What identity had I taken on with the discount of senior citizen? As the coach rattled on, I felt troubled and anxious, weighed down by the baggage of my new label. Was the saving worth the cost? The role itself seemed so constricting—senior citizen! Old fogey!—and reminded me of a story that my father used to tell about a village tailor known as Zumbach. As legend had it, a man in this village had succeeded in business and wanted to have a new suit made. He went to Zumbach, the most famous tailor in the land, and had himself measured. When he came back to Zumbach's shop the next week for the final fitting, put on his new suit and stood in front of the mirror, he saw that the right sleeve was two inches longer than the left.

"Er, Zumbach," he said, "there seems to be something wrong here. This sleeve is at least two inches too long."

The tailor, who didn't like backtalk from his customers, puffed himself up and said, "There is nothing wrong with the suit, my good man. Clearly, it's the way you're standing." With that, Zumbach pushed on the man's shoulder until the sleeves were even. But when the customer looked in the mirror, he saw that the fabric at the back of the suit was bunched up behind his neck. "Please, Zumbach," the poor man said, "my wife hates a suit that bulges in back. Would you mind just taking that out?"

Zumbach snorted indignantly, "I tell you there's nothing wrong with this suit! It must be the way you're standing." Zumbach shoved the man's head forward until the suit seemed to fit him to perfection. After paying the tailor's high price, the man left Zumbach's store in confusion.

Later that day, he was waiting at the bus stop with his shoulders lopsided and his head straining forward, when another fellow took hold of his lapel and said, "What a beautiful suit! I'll bet Zumbach the tailor made that suit for you."

"Why, yes," the man said, "but how did you know?"

"Because only a tailor as brilliant as Zumbach could outfit a body as crippled as yours."

The mantle of senior citizenship felt exactly like Zumbach's coat, and that very evening, on a train from Hartford to New York City, I began to seriously question where my ideas about aging had come from, why being old felt like such a stigma, and whether or not I could transform this process, with all the fears, losses, and uncertainties that came with it, from a necessary evil into an opportunity for spiritual and emotional growth. Was it possible to create a sort of curriculum for conscious aging? I'd spent a lot of time during the past thirty-five years working on issues of consciousness, after all; on developing a Soul perspective, rooted in spiritual wisdom. Now I wanted to take those decades of inner work and apply them to this new phase of life. But before I could discover an approach to aging unlike the one being offered by this culture (one that I'd absorbed without realizing it), I had to take a long, hard look at these cultural messages. I already knew from my work in sociology and psychology that the first step toward not being unconsciously influenced by something was to become conscious of it. Only by understanding the predicament could I begin to slip out of Zumbach's coat.

THE PREDICAMENT

Issues of sexuality, gender, and spirituality have come out of the closet since the Sixties. Because of midwives and hospices, even birth and death are out as well. Aging remains one of our culture's last taboos. Judging from how the old are represented (or rather, *not* represented) by the media, it's fair to say we live in a society that would like to pretend that old people don't exist. Since people typically spend less as they age, advertisers focus their attention on the young, unless they're selling denture adhesives or incontinence pads. A recent study showed that only three percent of the images seen in a day of television contains images of older people, and when you notice how these elders are depicted—as silly, stubborn, vindictive, or worst of all, *cute*—you begin to appreciate the not-so-subtle antipathy of a market-driven culture toward the elderly.

We cannot underestimate the media's influence on how we view ourselves as aging individuals. Men get trouble enough from the current obsession with staying young and beautiful, but women suffer even more from this craze. This is because men have traditionally had access to something almost as good as youth: power. Women have been deprived of this access until very recently. A man could be wrinkled and gray, but if he held high social or financial status, his physical losses were offset. Not so for women. Where an older man can be euphemized as "distinguished," a woman is more often called "faded" or "over the hill," and suffers enormous pressure to hide her age, often with painful results. Women now live a full third of their lives after menopause, and yet if you believe our popular culture, a woman who isn't young, shapely, and still capable of bearing children is all but invisible. I have women friends who've gone to great lengths to keep up a youthful front with the help of plastic surgery, and while the results may be superficially satisfying, the impulse to re-carve what nature has created often masks a profound despair. It is as if we are urged to fight, over and over again, a losing battle against time, pitting ourselves against natural law. How ghastly this is, and how inhumane, toward both ourselves and the cycle of life. It reminds me of someone rushing around the fields in the autumn painting the marvelous gold and red leaves with green paint. It's a lot of wasted time and energy.

Take the spots I have on my hands. Though I haven't been harmed by them at all, I am harmed by the message I see on TV. "They call these aging spots," an older woman says in a Porcelana ad, "but I call them ugly!" When I see that ad, I become uneasy about a natural process my body is going through. But when I flip that message around in my mind—"They call these ugly, I call them aging spots!"—the illusion is dispelled, and suddenly it's just autumn leaves.

I experienced this first-hand a few years back when I was invited to give a couple of talks for a company called La Prairie. It's a Swiss firm that makes a very fancy line of "age management" cosmetics. They heard that I'd been lecturing about aging, and thought that my presence might lend a transcendental touch to their products. Now ordinarily, I wouldn't be inclined to take on an assignment like that, since some might say that it compromised my role as a spiritual teacher to be concerned with such material things as keeping your body young and beautiful. But La Prairie had offered to pay me $6,000, which, in the service work our foundation supported doing cataract operations for the blind, represented a lot of eyeballs. So I said, "Why not?"

The plan was for me to speak at Saks Fifth Avenue in Beverly Hills to two hundred of the store's wealthiest clients. I was seated with the other speakers at a little table, where a skin nutritionist was going to tell us how to keep our skin lovely and supple. "We're going to do this little test," she said. "Let's all put our hands on the table in front of us, take a little pinch of skin and hold it for five seconds. Then we'll see how quickly it goes back into place. If it goes back down, you're in good shape. Otherwise, we have a problem!" With some trepidation, I put my hand out and pinched, but when I released, the skin just stayed there; in fact, if I hadn't pulled it back myself, it would be like that to this day. They all looked at me, appalled. How could I possibly be living that way? Afterward, they sent me huge jars of ointments and creams to help me recover my suppleness.

The images our culture generates are designed to make you feel that aging is a kind of failure; that somehow God made a big mistake. If God were as smart as the commercials, people would be young forever, but since God isn't, only the wonders of science and commerce can save us. Can you see how bizarre this assumption is, and how much pain it creates? Pitting ourselves more and more desperately against an inexorable process revealed in crow's feet, stretch marks and puffiness, we are given two equally doomed choices: to suck in, thrust out, tuck and nip, and build our muscles, all to hold onto a semblance of youth; or resign ourselves in sad defeat, feeling like failures, outsiders, victims, or fools.

The so-called *problem* of aging is trumpeted everywhere we turn. With the great wave of baby boomers moving into their 50s and 60s, the very economic stability of the United States is being called into question. There's the fear that Social Security will go bankrupt as more old people require support. In the eyes of the economists, the aged aren't merely a problem—we're a disaster. And we didn't do a thing!

If we listen to the rhetoric of the economists, politicians, social planners, advertisers, statisticians, and health-care providers, the overwhelming message we're sent is that aging is a great social ill, a necessary evil, a drain on society, and an affront to esthetics. When avoidance finally fails, old age should be coped with as one would cope with a chronic condition— leprosy, say, or an unwanted visitor who unpacks his bags and won't go away. We, the aging, are viewed as a burden instead of a resource. As Betty Friedan wrote in her own book on aging, "The old people begin to look like greedy geezers to the young, because (we're) costing the young so much, in so many ways."

This is a distorted view, of course, and not only a great disservice to the old but also one that inevitably returns to haunt the young. A Chinese story I love points this out beautifully. It tells of an old man who's too weak to work in the garden or help with household chores. He just sits on the porch, gazing out across the fields, while his son tills the soil and pulls up weeds. One day, the son looks up at the old man and thinks, "What good is he now that he's so old? All he does is eat up the food! I have a wife and children to think about. It's time for him to be done with life!" So he makes a large wooden box, places it on a wheelbarrow, rolls it up to the porch, and says to the old man, "Father, get in." The father lies down in the box and the son puts the cover on, then wheels it toward the cliff. At the edge of the cliff, the son hears a knock from inside the box. "Yes, father?" the son asks. The father replies, "Why don't you just throw me off the cliff and save the box? Your children are going to need it one day."

Unless we see ourselves as part of life's continuity, whether we're currently young or old, we will continue to view aging as something apart from the mainstream of culture, and the old as somehow *other*. In a non-traditional culture such as ours, dominated by technology, we value information far more than we do wisdom. But there is a difference between the two. Information involves the acquisition, organization, and dissemination of facts; a storing-up of physical data. But wisdom involves another equally crucial function: the emptying and quieting of the mind, the application of the heart, and the alchemy of reason and feeling. In the wisdom mode, we're not processing information, analytically or sequentially. We're standing back and viewing the whole, discerning what matters and what does not, weighing the meaning and depth of things. This quality of wisdom is rare in our culture. More often, we have knowledgeable people who pretend to be wise, but who, unfortunately, have not, cultivated the quality of mind from which wisdom truly arises.

When we spend time in traditional societies, where the young seek out the wisdom of their elders, we become aware of how upside-down such non-traditional values are. A few years ago I visited a village in India where I had spent a great deal of time. I visited the house of a dear friend, who said to me, "Oh, Ram Dass, you're looking so much older!" Because I live in the United States, my first reaction was defensive; inwardly, I thought to myself, "Gee, I thought I was looking pretty good." But when I paused to take in the tone of my friend's voice, this reaction melted instantly. I heard the respect with which he'd addressed me, as if to say, "You've done it, my friend! You've grown old! You've earned the respect due an elder now, someone we can rely on and to whom we can listen."

In a culture where information is prized over wisdom, however, old people become obsolete, like yesterday's computers. But the real treasure is being ignored: *wisdom is one of the few things in human life that does not diminish with age.* While everything else falls away, wisdom alone increases until death if we live examined lives, opening ourselves out to life's many lessons, rather than shrinking into Zumbach's coat. In traditional cultures that go unchanged for generation after generation, the value of wise elders is easy to spot; but in a culture such as ours, wisdom is nowhere near as exciting—or necessary—as surfing the Net. We feel we have to keep running to stay up-to-date, to learn the latest version of Windows or try out that Stairmaster at the gym. I used to have a sign over my computer that read OLD DOGS CAN LEARN NEW TRICKS, but lately I sometimes ask myself how many more new tricks I *want* to learn. How many more of those damned manuals do I want to read in this lifetime? Wouldn't it be easier just to be outdated?

Of course, it's not easy to be outdated—to move into the aging stage with grace and a sense of appropriateness—in a culture that does not value that metamorphosis or provide a respected role for its elders. Through the Omega Institute in New York, I have taken part with other colleagues in facilitating "Elder Circles." The oldest people in the group sit in a large circle, and the younger people sit just behind them. We use a talking stick, a custom adopted from a Native American tradition, and as they are ready, members of the inner circle can walk to the center, take the talking stick, return to their seats, and share their wisdom with the rest of the group. By custom, they begin their remarks with "And . . ." and end them with "I have spoken." This is an opportunity for people to share their own wisdom and to contribute it to the collective group wisdom. Many people flower in the richness of this process, as the group becomes aware of how each person holds some part of the complex mosaic that is elder wisdom. At the close of a circle, people have often said, "This is a role I'm totally unfamiliar with, because nobody's ever asked me to be wise before." It's impossible not to be moved by the poignancy of such a remark, as regards both the aging person and the culture deprived of such a precious resource.

If the situation is going to change, of course, it will be because we, the aging, work to change it. We cannot expect the young to beat down our doors, begging for our wisdom, reminding us of our responsibility to society. As older people, we will have to initiate the change by freeing ourselves of this culture's bias, and remember the unique things we bring to the table. As wise elders, we are capable of cultivating the very resources that our endangered world needs if it is to survive healthy and whole: qualities of sustainability, patience, reflection, appreciation for justice, and the humor born of long experience. These qualities are in short supply in our society.

Since the first baby boomers turned fifty in 1996, the opportunity has existed to right this imbalance and infuse our culture with elder wisdom. The American Association of Retired Persons (which one can join at age fifty) is already one of the most powerful lobbies in the United States. Numbers are power in a democracy, and the question we must ask ourselves now is, How do we want to use the power? Now that aging is coming out of the closet, how can we work toward increasing our culture's wisdom without hampering its devotion to progress? How can we work to reverse the "aging onus" that traps so many elderly people in the badly tailored suit of an outdated identity, blocking what they have to offer?

This is our predicament, then: to regain our roles as wise elders in a culture that has traditionally denied the need for wisdom, or the ability of the old to provide it; to envision a curriculum for aging with wisdom as its highest calling, and to use it as a means of enlightenment—our own, and that of the people around us. But it is futile to try to change the outside world without beginning with ourselves—as futile, said an Indian master, as trying to straighten out a dog's tail. It is futile as well to look for our "selves" without understanding how the self is defined by our culture, and by what we consider reality to be.

2

WHO
ARE
WE?

Although we are a religious nation, we are not, on close examination, an essentially spiritual one. While it is true that the Judeo-Christian values of charity, hard work, community, and so on do inform the shape and self-image of our culture, at root we are a secular society whose deepest leanings are toward the school of thought known as philosophical materialism. This label does not refer to our love affair with possessions and money; rather, philosophical materialism is the idea that reality is limited to what we perceive through our senses. If something cannot be seen, smelled, tasted, heard, or touched with our physical bodies, or measured by experimental means in a laboratory, materialism posits that it does not exist except as a creation of the mind. Although non-material (extrasensory) phenomena are allowed to exist in the sphere of religion, our view of "everyday" reality is mostly divorced from the realm of spirit. We use science as our bottom line, our gauge for determining what is real and what is not. Though it is common knowledge in spiritual cultures that the mind cannot measure phenomena that exist beyond the mind, our culture tends to disregard the possibility that there is any reality beyond our senses. In spite of our churchgoing status (ninety percent of Americans claim belief in some version of God), and the infiltration of Eastern and New Age thought since the late Fifties and Sixties, Americans remain by and large a people with their hearts in Missouri, the "Show Me State." "Show me," we say, "and then I'll believe it."

Well, maybe I can help you show yourself something. There's a lot that we can't see that we never would have believed a couple of centuries ago: atoms, quarks, jet propulsion, whole galaxies, and we couldn't have dreamed of the microscopes and telescopes we now have for observing all these things. The Sufi Mulah Nasrudin reminds us that looking for reality only through the lens of science is like a drunkard losing his keys in the dark and only looking around the lamppost because that's where he can see. Science tells us that the universe is made of matter and energy. A Tibetan friend of mine, Gelek Rinpoche, would challenge us on that. He says that the universe is made of matter, energy and consciousness. How can we deny this when we encounter the existence of our own and others' consciousness every single day? And how can we assume that consciousness is annihilated just because the body, the matter, gives out? Matter and energy are not destroyed—just converted into each other. I'll bet that consciousness can't be destroyed either.

The belief that nothing exists beyond what we can see, taste, touch, hear, or experience has wide-ranging effects, but none more critical than how we view the cycles of our lives, from birth through maturity, aging, and death. For people who view life only through the senses, death is the obvious end of the road; beyond the demise of our physical bodies, they say, nothing exists. For people of faith, other planes may exist as realms apart from our earthly sphere, and although our activities may affect the future, the afterlife remains speculative, without direct influence on how we view our earthly existence. According to this material view, we are separate, finite entities living in a world of changing phenomena, waiting for our annihilation. So it's no great surprise that death and its friends, sickness and old age, have been sources of such dread in this culture, and are so terribly misunderstood. If we begin to open our minds, however, recognizing the degree to which this kind of thinking has influenced us, we're able to think outside this box and take a quite different view of the process of aging.

In spite of problems in public health, civil rights, and the economy, and taking into consideration the Coca-Cola-ization of the subcontinent, there remains in India an unbroken metaphysical tradition whose understanding of aging and death can help us tremendously in our current predicament. Hinduism looks at existence from a broader perspective than a single lifetime. What pervades Indian culture is the understanding that the Soul continues after death. The *Atman* is God, the Awareness in which the Soul yearns to abide. This non-physical, non-material aspect of human life is as real to Indians of various faiths as are their bodies and minds, which leads them to view death not as the end of the road, but as a point of transition, and their physical lives as a stage in the ongoing journey of the Soul toward self-realization. This view can work as a two-edged sword, of course, creating a certain indifference toward the things of the earth; one glance at India's physical ills is enough to make clear the danger of giving too much value to future lives and not enough to survival or the material plane. But metaphysical Awareness helps as well by reducing the stress of our twin nemeses: the compulsion to "have it all" now, and the desperate clinging to things of the past, including our youth. Emphasis is placed on eternal matters, which relieves the suffering of fighting against nature. And because the goal is God, rather than thin thighs, fabulous pensions, and geriatric erections, the old in India enjoy a peace, after the storm of youth, that is largely unknown to aging Americans. Many of us spend our lives worrying about losing what we have. Old age offers the opportunity to shift our cares away from the physical toward what cannot be taken away: our wisdom and the love we offer to those around us. But a culture without spiritual underpinnings deprives us of this opportunity. What Indians experience as a time of liberation is experienced by many Americans as a time of loss.

In a materialistic culture, the body and its longevity take on paramount importance. Thanks to technology and medical advances, the average life expectancy has increased by twenty-five years during this century alone; we can only imagine what the next hundred years will bring. If we believe that we are only the body, then keeping it alive is the ultimate goal and ideal, and in spite of Ambrose Bierce's observation that "longevity is an uncommon extension of the fear of death," Americans have followed this course with some painful consequences. When a culture creates its mythology, for example, it does so on the basis of given circumstances; in this case, how long we can expect to live. But mythology changes more slowly than facts, which is why, as a larger segment of the population lives into "old age," people find themselves with no mythology to support their presence, no *place*—figurative or otherwise—for themselves in the culture. Yet the urgency to keep our bodies alive for as long as possible is undeniable. This reminds me of a comment made by a French woman, the oldest living person on record, when she was asked on her birthday what she expected the future to be like. "Very short," she replied.

None of this is new, of course. Many cultures before ours have dreamt of the fountain of youth and searched for the elixir of immortality. And I am not knocking longevity per se.

A long life is also a great opportunity to do spiritual practice—if you're reading this book, it means you have the time and opportunity, and this life is the best kind of life for developing the qualities that help move the Soul along in its evolution. But we have to do two things while investigating our own attitudes toward aging: First, look at the underlying question of whether we believe ourselves to be bodies with brain-centered minds and nothing more; and second, ask ourselves, "Can there ever be enough?" In a society focused on the physical and psychological planes, more always appears to be better: more time, more health, more experiences, more possessions. We must examine whether more is indeed better, and when, if ever, enough is enough.

In the late Sixties, I was invited to speak at a hotel in New Hampshire—one of those old, very fancy, Jewish summer hotels. In the fashion of that time and milieu, the women were heavily coiffured and made up, with blue eyelids and black mascara, wearing the semi-transparent bathing suits in vogue then. The men were smoking cigars about a foot long, lying back in their deck chairs, puffing and portly.

I remember saying to them, "Well, you've really made it, haven't you? Look at where you've ended up. You're at one of the best hotels in the country. The parking lot is full of Cadillacs—even a few Rolls-Royces. You have your children in private schools. You have money in the bank. Many of you have two homes. You have all the physical comforts you could ask for." The people in the audience were all smiles, happy and self-satisfied. And then I said simply, "Is it enough?"

My question had opened a Pandora's box of painful feelings and doubts that took us into a deep discussion of where our cultural myth had failed us by promising that we would be happy as we got older if only we accrued enough comfort, and if we didn't pause to ask ourselves when, if ever, this striving could end. By identifying so strongly with their bodies and physical possessions, the people in that audience had come to believe that they *were* the sum of their material lives, and it only took a moment's insight to make them realize how much suffering this belief had created. Worldly success had not brought the rewards it had promised—of peace, serenity, at-homeness, well-being—and several people mentioned that they felt like they'd "been had." They'd won, they said, and yet they were losing.

Though few of us enjoy material comfort on that level, we find ourselves in the same predicament, seeking our self-worth and the meaning of our lives and deaths only through our jobs, what we possess, and the state of our physical bodies. Though many Americans proclaim a faith in God, their spiritual lives are restricted to church, or temple, or mosque, and rarely, if ever, applied to the question of aging. We are deprived of the freedom that Buddhists, educated in laws of impermanence, or Hindus familiar with the presence of *jivatman* (Soul) receive from their spiritual education. If we consider a model of reality expanded beyond philosophical materialism, however—one closer to what Aldous Huxley termed the "perennial philosophy"—we can begin to view the aging process in a radically different light.

THE THREE LEVELS OF BEING

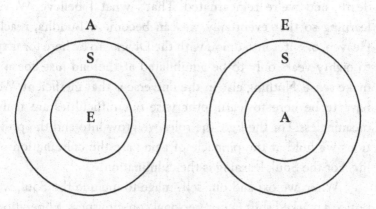

A = *AWARENESS/ATMAN*
S = *SOUL*
E = *EGO*

The diagram on the left, with the Ego on the outside, is how we usually approach the world: me first. The Ego realm includes all of the things we experience as "ourselves" on the psycho-physical plane: our physical bodies, our personalities, fame, reputation, possessions, emotions, and the conceptual structures within our minds that develop to help us function here. The Ego, to borrow Descartes' famous saying, is made of who "we think" we are: a body-mind of a certain age, with certain tastes, desires, opinions. Peering out at the world, this Ego sees only other Egos, separate, sensory beings, and takes as its "operating system" what science is able to explain, with the brain "computer" its sole conveyor.

But Ego is a tiny thing in the sea of Awareness, as you can see in the diagram on the right. Beyond Ego lies the Soul. The Soul is here to learn, and aging and all its inevitable difficulties are a prime learning opportunity. But what are we going through all this learning for? The future, of course. Peace of mind now and later. Much later. I know this is going to give everyone trouble, but I'll come right out and say it. The Soul transcends death, and we're reincarnated. That's what I believe. We're learning so that eventually we can become a Buddha, reach Heaven, or enter into union with the Divine. To be here for fifty to eighty years only to be annihilated at the end just doesn't make sense. Nothing else in the universe is that inefficient. We have to be here to learn; otherwise our difficulties are truly meaningless. For the Ego, the roles we grow into and the positions we hold at the pinnacle of aging are the culmination of life. For the Soul, learning is the culmination.

When we expand our self-image to include the Soul, we notice a marked shift in our personal consciousness, a liberation from the small egotistical self into a far more spacious context. From this Soul level, we are able to view our Egos from the outside in. This allows us to observe our minds and bodies in ways that will seem new and surprising, as if the trapdoors of the "self" have been opened and we can finally step outside, enjoy the view, and put a welcome distance between who we are (from Soul's perspective) and the suffering we experience at the level of body and mind. Thus, with practice, we cultivate the tremendous healing of knowing ourselves as spiritual beings, too.

As the wave is not the ocean, however, the Soul is not the extent of consciousness. Beyond the Soul level lies the very Ground of Being, which I've termed Awareness (A) in our diagram on the right. In the diagram on the left, you can see that Awareness is trapped by the constructs of Ego. You will notice that while the Soul and Ego are contained within the level of Awareness, Awareness itself has no outer boundary, being eternal and infinite. There are many words used to describe this all-inclusive domain: God, *Brahma*, *Paramatman*, the Nameless, the Formless, the Unmanifest, the Nondual, the Absolute. Ego and Soul are inextricable parts of Awareness, just as Awareness is the very essence of who we are. This leap from self to Awareness is difficult for the Ego to make, however. It signifies the mystical union experienced by saints and described by poets, in which the separate self is left behind and dissolved into God, going home to what we really are.

The Ego is what experiences aging and death. It doesn't continue, but it is nearly impossible for the Ego to imagine its own demise. When the Ego thinks it's dying, it mistakes itself for the whole—body, Soul and Awareness—and often people who are beginning to go through the long process of ripening into God run around to different doctors (and maybe even shrinks) because they develop an even more intense dread of death.

Awareness, God, whatever you want to call it, is beyond time and concept. This is the Ground of Being. Souls explode out of Awareness like little Big Bangs. The Soul's relationship to Awareness is like child to mother. The clear light of Awareness is what the Soul yearns to return to. Ripening into God is the Soul's journey.

There is a wonderful exercise, found in the Tibetan Dzogchen practice, for entering the Awareness plane of consciousness It's called sky-gazing. Lie down on your back, look up at the sky, and watch the clouds pass over. After a while, you begin to experience the sky as mirroring the sky of your own Awareness. In time, you start to *be* the sky, with the clouds becoming the phenomena that enter your mind and body—desires, fears, images, sounds, smells, all of it. The sky doesn't pay attention to the clouds passing through. It just stays open as they all go by.

What we require, in order to re-imagine the process of getting older as a healing path, is simply the knowledge that we are more than our bodies and minds. Realizing that the Ego is merely a fragment of who we are comes as a shock to the system at first. But once we've begun to experience Soul consciousness in daily life, we find that it offers great relief from the pain, fear, loss, anger, and other difficult mind-states that arise with aging. Soul Awareness offers a way of stepping back from our physical and mental states and viewing who we are with wisdom and spaciousness. This practice requires humility and patience. Though I've been involved in spiritual practice for nearly four decades, I backslide into my old habits on a daily basis; still, the willingness to open our eyes to the possibility of our larger Self can transform our aging process into a spiritual opportunity.

3

OLD MIND,
NEW MIND

When I first began to explore altered states of consciousness back in the Sixties, through exposure to entheogens such as LSD, and the enlightened presence of my guru, Neem Karoli Baba (Maharajji), it came as a shock to realize how limited my ideas were about what my mind was and how it worked. I realized that what I was accustomed to calling "reality" was, more accurately, my subjective perception of things, and what's more, that *I was capable of changing that perception.* I realized that the suffering I experienced as a result of perceived reality was, to a large degree, self-induced, and could be shifted by watching my thoughts, and moving from my Ego to a Witness perspective. With the help of my guru, meditation practice, and chemical teachers, this Awareness has strengthened over the years and helped me tremendously in the process of learning to age.

Let's pause for a moment to look more closely at what I've called self-induced suffering. Please understand that I am not for a moment denying the very real difficulties and pain of aging, the challenges faced by millions of people shut out from family and proper employment, adequate health care, and community; nor am I making light of the physical troubles that come our way as the body loses its youth. But there is a fundamental difference between pain and suffering, as we'll see; a difference that involves our minds, and how we react to experience.

We know that in a materialistic culture, the outer world

takes on primary importance. Although we have some control over our external circumstances, we realize that this control is limited, and that there are aspects of our lives that we can't change—taxes, for instance; the behavior of our children; or the fact that we will age and die. Since we are not able to keep bad things from happening to us, reason concludes that we are life's victims or her fools, struggling creatures with limited power, fighting a losing battle with nature. From the time we're old enough to realize that life offers things that we wish were different, we're taught that we are captives of circumstance, that outer reality has the final say in who we are, how we feel, what we think, and what is possible.

Like most of our fundamental assumptions, this version of reality sounds true. But does it tell the entire story? Prick your skin and it will bleed, spend your money and you will be broke. But when bad things happen, does this mean that we have to be completely depressed about them? We can see reality from different angles, so we can choose how we wish to respond to events. We tend to forget the flexibility of our own minds. We allow ourselves to be controlled by our experience, believing that if such-and-such happens, we must behave in certain customary or habitual ways. As we age, we believe what we're trained to believe about how old people think and live. The Ego gets us to view ourselves as something less than we were when young, rather than something more. And yet we have the power to age *as we choose*, and to use our changing circumstances to benefit the world and ourselves, if we take the time to know the mind and how it determines the quality of life.

It is the mind, the Ego, far more than outer circumstances, that creates our suffering. You see this often when working with people who are ill. Over the years, I've met individuals diagnosed with the same illness who've reacted to it in nearly opposite ways. Take Elaine. When this sixty-three-year-old retired schoolteacher was told that she had lymphoma, which required chemotherapy that offered her a less-than-fifty-percent survival prognosis, she did not let it stop her life. A deeply religious woman, she was able, after the initial shock and depression had passed, to heal the non-physical aspects of her life—including an unhappy marriage—at the same time that she was taking her cancer treatment, thus highly reducing the pain of her condition. "I saw that I had a choice," Elaine told me. "Change my mind or stop living." While circumstances could be used to justify a retreat from inner growth and the state of her mind, Elaine used her diagnosis as an opportunity for conscious healing that provided insight during a difficult time. By learning to step back out of the Ego's fear of death into Soul Awareness, and to separate difficult feelings from physical pain, we're able to reduce our suffering a little more.

In this same way, it is not the phenomena of aging that create suffering, but how the mind deals with these phenomena. For example, I've noticed an epidemic of "if only-itis" in my work with people confronting old age. "If only I didn't live here, I could do that." "If only such-and-such were not my lot, I could have such-and-such that would make me happy." But these "if onlys" are the Ego's self-sabotage, and keep older people trapped in longings, in clinging to what-could-be, unable to rest in the present moment. As we age and lose the things of this world, and find ourselves less able to change our external circumstances, this list of "if onlys" is bound to get longer, and our feelings of powerlessness will continue to grow with it.

As we quiet down and move inward with age, we realize how vital it is to use our minds in ways that liberate us from the traps of the past. Luckily, old age provides us with ample opportunity to learn these new lessons. Many retired people find themselves with too much time on their hands. With the trumpets of desire quieting down, and worldly pursuits starting to fall away, you have the opportunity to spend more quality time with yourself, and to understand the power of your own mind.

One of the simplest methods I know of for working with the mind is mindfulness meditation, which I have been practicing since 1970. Although this technique derives from the Theravadin Buddhist tradition, it is not necessary to be a Buddhist to benefit greatly from its rewards, nor does it require faith, religious devotion, or metaphysical leanings of any kind. Mindfulness practice simply invites us to become acquainted with our own minds, using the breath as an object of focus. Most of the great spiritual traditions include some version of mindfulness practice. I believe that these practices are meant to help us begin to step back from our Egos, and begin to live from the Soul perspective.

INSTRUCTIONS ON
MINDFULNESS PRACTICE

One of the best ways of checking out how the Ego is controlling us and causing suffering is to learn to be here now. Easier said than done, because the Ego will come up with a million ways to distract us. It has very good survival instincts, so it knows when we're trying to catch it at its own game. It does not want to lose its "king of the hill" game to the Soul.

Getting the Ego to release its grip can be as simple as being able to experience what's present at any given time. It sounds simple, but volumes have been written about just how to do this, some of them thousands of years old. It's called meditation, and can be done on the cushion or off the cushion—in other words, simply while living.

To get started, let's just sit down somewhere and be comfortable. If you're in a chair, let your feet rest flat on the ground, and let your hands rest on your legs. Try not to slump, but don't hold yourself rigidly either. If you need to, close your eyes and think about relaxing each part of your body separately. Visualize your body and mind entering into a state of being at ease. If you want to sit on the ground, that's fine, but make sure you're not straining anything. If you've never done this before, and you're not used to twisting your body into a pretzel, I recommend a chair. You don't want to begin to associate meditation with pain.

To bring the mind home to seeing what's here now, we can begin with resting part of our attention on the breath, the rise and fall of the abdomen, the air going in and out of the nostrils, the expansion and contraction of the lungs. Relax the jaw, keep your lips together and your tongue touching the roof of your mouth just behind the top teeth. You can keep your eyes closed, or you can leave them slightly open, and look down at about a forty-five-degree angle, but not focused on anything in particular.

When we try to rest the attention on the breath, we notice a couple of things. First, we'll hold on to the breath either too tightly or too loosely. We'll concentrate all our effort on breathing, or we'll fall asleep. We'll breathe deliberately instead of naturally. Then we'll get caught in a thought and we'll be off to India, the office, a fight we had last week with a loved one, a happy birthday memory, the hopes for tomorrow night's dinner plans. That's normal. That's the Ego coming in and getting us caught up in its ideas of how things should be. The Ego weakens every time we let go of the thought or the distraction and bring ourselves back to the breath.

The silence, during moments like these, can be deafening, as they say, or it can become a very big space for the Soul to rest in and to begin to perceive things just as they are. Our insides will seem noisier than ever, and it can make the outside seem more irritating than ever. Nothing has changed but our attitudes.

The most important thing, when you get distracted from the breath or find yourself no longer resting in an Awareness that accepts all the sounds, feelings in the body, or thoughts as they pass through, is not to get mad at yourself. Meditating like this is hard to do. When we were babies and learned to walk, we fell a lot but we kept getting back up. At our stage of life, the most important thing we can do is to help the Soul learn how to walk in Awareness. The Ego will knock it down a lot, but if you keep helping it get back up, you will get it, and you will be able to find a great deal of peace.

One thing you will notice as you begin your mindfulness practice is how out of control your mind is! If this is your first experience of watching the mental process carefully, you may be appalled by what you see. No sooner have you closed your eyes than you are bombarded by images, feelings, and body sensations. Each time we pay attention to the mind, and become more conscious, we enable the Soul to step in and keep us from getting caught in the Ego's habits. This can be done anywhere at any time—sitting quietly in nature, in church or temple, or simply while looking at the sky. Whatever method you choose will be of great help in facing the worries about what's to come. Once we have developed a little calmness from meditation, we can begin to face the mind's catalog of demons and see them as only an invention of the mind. The demons I'm interested in talking about are the usual fears about aging.

Senility

I remember visiting my eighty-six-year-old aunt in the hospital. Our conversation went something like this:

She: "What's your name?"

Me: "Richard."

She: "Who's your father?"

Me: "Your brother George."

She: "Oh, yes, yes." (long pause) "Are you and I the same age?"

Me: "No."

She: "Am I older than you?"

Me: "Yes, you're thirty years older than I am."

She: "*Thirty years* older? But you're all gray!"

Me: "So are you!"

She: (long pause) "What did you say your name was?"

And around we'd go again. My aunt was just floating out there, with little connection to time or personal relationships. Most often, I just held her hand, and we looked into each other's eyes. It didn't matter that she couldn't remember me; she didn't seem particularly anxious about it. We were just two beings meeting in Soul time together, and once I'd released my attachment to speaking to her on the Ego level, both of us enjoyed our visits immensely.

Because we are so identified with our thoughts and feelings, and so sure that they and only they tell us who we really are, it's very hard for us not to panic when our minds slip. And yet there are cases in which what we call senility is, in fact, a process that need not be so frightening. As Frances, a resident in a nursing home, said, "Lack of physical strength keeps me inactive and often silent. They call me senile, but senility is just a convenient peg on which to hang non-conformity. A new set of faculties seems to be coming into operation. More than at any other time of my life, I seem to be aware of the beauties of our spinning planet and the sky above. Old age is sharpening my Awareness." In other words, what appears to be loss may in fact be transformation, if we allow the mind to change without fear.

There is an award-winning film, "Complaints of a Dutiful Daughter," that I love for its honesty and its ability to awaken. The writer-director chronicles the advancing stages of Alzheimer's Syndrome in her mother, at the same time recording her own reactions to this illness. The disease progresses until at last the mother no longer recognizes her daughter at all. Finally, when it becomes too dangerous for the mother to remain in her own apartment, the daughter moves her to a nursing home for patients with Alzheimer's.

During the admissions process, the head of the nursing home tells the daughter not to leave anything from the past with her mother—not even her clothes. This seems harsh at the time, but the daughter does as she's asked. When she returns the next day, she finds her mother wearing a man's sweatsuit, and carrying a pocketbook with one penny in it. The daughter suddenly realizes that her mother is quite happy, now that there's no one around to remind her of what she's forgotten. The daughter realizes that her loving attachment to the mother she's known has only prolonged her mother's suffering. In time, she learns to relax her attachment and to dance with her mother's consciousness wherever it might flow. In the last scene, the mother is walking down the corridor, swinging her pocketbook, and singing, "I'm freeee. I'm freeee!"

When we begin to examine the contents of our minds, we discover a cluster of common demons—what I call The Usual Suspects—that cause us trouble as we grow older. The first of these is senility—or the fear of losing our mental faculties.

Nothing, save physical incapacitation, is more daunting than the prospect of senility. Before I had my stroke, losing my mental acuity was certainly at the top of my own list. But once we've tasted Soul Awareness, we find that whether or not we've got all our marbles almost doesn't matter. Soul Awareness is so much bigger than mental Awareness and once you have it, it's yours forever.

Of course, the loss of one's mind isn't always so simple. For many people, as the structures of Ego-mind dissolve, a lot of ill-digested psychological stuff surfaces that may involve tremendous agitation, anger-filled delusions, or even violence. A very conscious woman who had been caring for her husband of fifty-four years through the progression of his Alzheimer's Syndrome, and doing it with grace, wrote to tell me that her husband was now in a group home. She told me that her husband had become lost in frightening sexual delusions. He thought that he was in a whorehouse, and that she was a madam who was forcing him to have sex with two dozen girls at once; to escape, he tried to climb out through the window of their high-rise apartment. The wife went to him to save him, but he saw her as the madam, and struck her when she attempted to hold him back. The previous week he had pushed her out of bed, saying it was improper for a man to sleep with his sister. Much as she wanted to continue to be with him, his state of mind, and the actions it generated, were too much for her to handle.

For most of us, however, the *fear* of losing our minds—rather than brain-related disease—will be our primary challenge. Like all difficult mind-states, however, this fear contains the seeds of its own healing. Mindfulness practice reveals that what we call "fear" is not an insurmountable obstacle, but rather a thought—or series of thoughts—accompanied by physical sensation. Fearful thoughts arise most commonly due to our tendency to dwell in the past or invent the future. "If this bad thing that happened a year ago happens again, what will I do?" we worry. With the future always unknown, the fearful mind is free to create a horror-show of catastrophes, each leading to the next in a snowball of ever-growing panic. There is no end to unchecked fear; as we get older and feel more vulnerable in the world, fear in its myriad forms can become a chronic companion that renders old age a living hell.

If, however, we choose a path of the Soul, we discover a capacity to work with these fears rather than become their victims. When I speak of "working," I don't mean willing the Ego into resistance, but of remaining alert to the signs of fear's presence in the mind. When we become aware that fear is present, we bring whatever clarity, quiet, and attention we can to the thought(s) that may be prompting the fear—a rise in the cost of food, for example, or some new physical challenge—and notice where our mind is attached. It is the mental tendency to cling that creates anxiety, suffering, and fear, and once we're able to identify what we are attached to—a certain standard of living, say, or a body that does not change—we are able to take the first steps toward freeing ourselves, regardless of the particular difficulty.

Loneliness

Loneliness is another frequent complaint of aging people (and one which we will discuss at great length in our chapter on Shifting Roles and Relationships). I can remember many painful moments throughout my life when I have felt completely cut off from other people, isolated, abandoned, unloved, friendless, as if there was nobody to turn to. In those moments, which so many of us experience later in life, I've felt as if I could drown in my own loneliness. These feelings have dimmed with time, now that I'm surrounded with caregivers, but their memory remains vivid. Like "Eleanor Rigby" in the song by the Beatles, many of us endure our old age and death in isolation.

Though we may not be able to change our physical circumstances, we can do a great deal to alleviate the suffering of such loneliness. Our first step is to remain alert to the earliest hint of that lonely feeling arising within us. As with all self-healing, the more quickly we become aware of a mind-state, the more effective our mindfulness practice will be in alleviating it. Once you are aware of this loneliness, begin to quiet yourself and be the witness of loneliness. You will notice that although your feelings of loneliness may remain, their intensity will diminish. The Ego will no longer be milking the mind-state for drama: "Oh, woe is me, I'm so very lonely, the loneliest person on earth!" When we do this, we just feed our loneliness and prolong our suffering. Notice that there is no denial of the lonely feelings, simply a shift in consciousness from the Ego to the Soul, allowing you to feel *what is*, without taking on the suffering. The great capacity of the Soul is that it accepts whatever is without trying to push it away.

Even the loneliest people among us are not lonely all the time, and a certain degree of mindfulness allows us to remember this in difficult moments. Be aware of the Ego's reflexive desire to cling (even to negative experience). You may also feel compelled to relieve the loneliness by whatever means possible. Be aware that you can obey such impulses or not, and that the feeling will pass like weather if you allow it to.

There is a big difference between being lonely and being alone. Loneliness is an affair of the Ego. Being alone can be a moment for the Soul. It is necessary to be alone to have the time to be quiet, to meditate, to get to know ourselves. The Soul cannot grow into Awareness if the Ego keeps us busy with other people, activities, or worrying about how lonely we are. Being alone is a great opportunity.

But in another sense, we are never alone. We may not know these people, but no matter where we are or how miserable we're feeling, there is probably someone nearby who feels the same way. Reach out to that person through your Soul. Think about what it might feel like to be that other person, suffering from loneliness with no mindfulness practice to help. Think about all the people who might be suffering, just like you. They are present, in bodies, on the planet, just like you. If you were to wish that their suffering, and yours, could be eased, you might feel a little loosening. One way to sneak the Soul in past the Ego is through compassion. Not pity, but compassion: the genuine wish for the suffering of others to cease. When it can't worry about itself, the Ego becomes powerless to feed its own fears.

We can use our developing Awareness to completely transform loneliness. As you dwell in Awareness, you begin to taste the Great Aloneness—the Aloneness of there being only one Awareness in the universe. Aloneness of God becomes apparent, you become part of the Great Aloneness that includes everything. Loneliness changes into aloneness, and that feeling connects us with God.

Embarrassment

Embarrassment is another mind-state we frequently encounter as we get older. Let me tell you a personal story. A few years back, I was invited to speak to an audience of several thousand people in Denver, Colorado. I sat in the front row of the hall as the host sang my praises, and when it came time for me to take the stage, rather than climb the steps like most sixty-three-year-olds would, my Ego, inflated from too much praise, urged me to leap from the floor to the podium. The next thing I knew I was flat on my face in front of this crowd, my leg mangled and bleeding. Rather than attend to my needs, I lectured for the next hour with blood dripping down into my sock, too embarrassed to admit that I was ready to pass out.

Looking back on that experience, I'm amazed by the force of my own Ego, and how it controlled me in that situation. Rather than stopping the lecture for a few minutes to have my cut cleaned and bandaged—as I would have done had I been more conscious—I allowed myself to "become" the embarrassment, so to speak, and give it complete domination. Behind the embarrassment I felt over falling was the embarrassment I felt about getting older, and my embarrassment about my embarrassment! I had been embarrassed to take the stairs placed there for someone my age, and this prevented me from behaving appropriately under the circumstances. Such lapses in judgment were quite common for me in my 50s and 60s; perhaps because I tended to overlook my body, I was more prone to overestimating its powers. Or perhaps I was simply more arrogant. In any case, it is fascinating now to discover that the embarrassment I felt over getting older has nearly disappeared with my physical disability. Back then, I was worried about not looking fit. Since the stroke I have been wheelchair-bound, and unable to do simple things like roll over at night while in bed. This was much harder to take at the beginning. It gets easier as the Ego lets go of its concerns.

T. S. Eliot wrote: "Getting older, you refuse to fritter away your time on nonsense You drop your masks, your little vanities and false ambitions." He hadn't known my mother. I was alone with her one day in her hospital room a few days before she passed away. She was very weak, but with what little remaining strength she had, she held a fan in front of her mouth so that I wouldn't see her without her dentures. Her gums had become so sensitive that she could no longer wear her false teeth, and nobody but my father and her dentist was permitted to see her without them. What's worse, the steroids she received during her treatment had caused some hair growth on her face, and I watched her scour her skin with tweezers many times lest anyone see a hair or two. Mother was at war with the ways in which illness and treatment were changing her body, and this conflict, born of embarrassment, prevented her from being at peace. It was a losing battle in the end, but she could not stop waging it. She'd been trained by her culture to be this way and had learned the lesson all too well. Even my old friend Timothy Leary kept his mouth clamped shut as people shot photographs of him during his final illness. A closed mouth was not characteristic of Tim and when I asked him what was going on, he opened his mouth to show me that a few of his teeth were missing in front. This was not an image that he wished to project; in other words, he was embarrassed.

An old Chinese woman doctor I know had a delightful attitude about her teeth. When asked one day why she looked different, she opened her face into a huge smile and said, "I today Halloween!" You could see clearly that she only had four teeth left, all in different corners of her mouth. She just giggled and said they were hurting her and she didn't need them anymore so she had them taken out. "I lose my teeth just like my grandma," she said, and went on treating her patients.

Less than a year after my mother's death, I was on the other side of the world in India, sitting before Neem Karoli Baba, who was in his late seventies and of considerable girth. He had only three teeth, two of which were in the back of his mouth, and he held no fan—in fact, there seemed to be no self-consciousness whatsoever about his obesity or his dental condition. We devotees sat there hour after hour, feasting our eyes on the beauty of his being.

The same lack of self-consciousness was true of Anandamayi Ma, considered by many to be the greatest female saint of this century. When I sat with her toward the end of her life, this teacher, who'd once been a ravishing beauty, seemed unconcerned with how decrepit her body had become. Her luminosity emanated from deep within her and infused her toothless smile and wrinkled hands with a beauty that transcended the physical form. It was the beauty of a Soul shining through a threadbare veil.

Powerlessness

In our practice of mindfulness, we learn to distinguish among the levels of our own being. By identifying ourselves with the Soul, we enable ourselves to age with humble strength and peace of spirit.

Many aging people complain of a sense of powerlessness in their lives, not only due to diminished physical strength—and the fear of not being able to defend themselves in an aggressive world—but powerlessness against other changes that come with the years, which sometimes confuse us. This may lead to increasing distrust and anxiety, and to the tendency to view the world around us as foe rather than friend. A few years back, I spent several hours with a group of residents of an upscale senior community, ranging in age from sixty-five to eighty-five. They were a delightful group of fifteen or so, and as we got to know each other, they shared their experiences of being inside their protected environment. One gentleman described the seven-story building in which they lived as their own private cruise ship. This sounded pleasant enough, though the prospect of being on a permanent vacation, adrift in a private, self-enclosed world, was vaguely disturbing. The times I'd spent on ocean liners were enjoyable because they were brief, and I'd always been happy to disembark. But a far more disturbing comment came from a woman who told me in a quavering voice about how frightened she was of leaving the building because of what she saw on TV, referring to the violence "out there."

Suddenly, that retirement community changed in my eyes from *The Love Boat* to a fortress protected from hordes of marauders by a security moat. Though the street outside the room where we sat was calm and nearly deserted, this lady imagined danger waiting nearby to pounce on her if she ventured out. This is an extreme case of what happens when you make your world smaller. When you shrink your world to your immediate surroundings, you end up trapped by them. This woman's fearful confession broke my heart; it was clear to me that although crime does exist in the world, the marauders were inside her own mind. She had locked herself up in a very small place, physically and mentally, due to a feeling of powerlessness. By closing herself off to the possibilities lying just beyond her way of thinking, she'd deprived herself of vital tools and wisdom that could help her live a happier life. Had I been able to persuade her to accompany me to a soup kitchen to help feed the homeless, for example, this fearsome idea of "us" versus "them" might have been relieved a little, empowering this dear lady and helping her feel less vulnerable.

This claustrophobic vision is not the inevitable outcome of old age. Maggie Kuhn, the feisty founder of the Gray Panthers, traveled the world as an activist in her 80s. And Father Tom Berry, the brilliant deep ecologist, never allowed his physical frailty to interfere with his work in the world. He devoted himself specifically to helping our culture become more mindful of the way it is destroying the planet. Both Maggie and Tom found useful ways of transcending themselves, but while they have taken on public roles, this isn't necessary at all; what matters is our intention to step beyond our perceived limitations.

Not all limitations are self-imposed, as I've learned from this stroke. And yet, regardless of the extent to which we may be disabled, mindfulness remains possible, provided our minds are capable of focus. In fact, and here's the paradox, the secret of spiritual practice is that our limits may become our strengths if we learn to work with them skillfully. Similarly, as our bodies slow down, we can use this change to increase our mindfulness.

Loss of Role/Meaning

Along with the feeling of powerlessness that many people experience with age can come a loss of meaning—the belief that as the roles to which we've become accustomed (worker, parent, consumer, lover) change, we cease to matter as individuals. Such painful feelings of meaninglessness, and the depression they often engender, deprive us of joy and lead us to see ourselves as burdensome and obsolete. Often when I've visited nursing homes where the corridors were filled with old people shuffling along in bedroom slippers or seated in wheelchairs along the walls, I've come across a common question: Why are we still alive in these useless old bodies? This is a heartrending question to hear from old people who, in most other cultures of the world, would be the pride and joy of their communities, while in our own they are outcasts.

Instead of honor and tender care, many of our aging population experience boredom, despair and emptiness, with no outlet for their suffering. *It is important that we not wait until we find ourselves at such an impasse before seeking an alternative means of confronting our aging years.* The sooner we begin cultivating a mind that can work with such heavy mental states as meaninglessness and depression, the better able we will be, later on, to escape them. Again, we can begin by noting our thoughts as they arise, and by prying loose the Ego's hold, slowly, diligently, with great care. As our minds begin to quiet down, we notice that the thoughts and feelings associated with meaninglessness come and go, and that there exists, in the space between these arisings, a way of being that is not affected by these mind-states. The Soul, we discover, seeks no meaning; its "meaning," to borrow that Ego-concept, is self-evident. A flower does not question its meaning or right to exist; it simply *is*, and its purpose is joy. In one of his most exquisite essays, Emerson compares our human attachment to meaning, and to history, thus: "These roses under my window make no reference to former roses or to better ones; they are for what they are; they exist with God today. There is no time to them. There is simply the rose; it is perfect in every moment of its existence."

While this may seem too simple—we are not flowers, after all—it contains a profound truth as well that we tend to forget in our complex lives. Before we are parents, executives, or neighborhood activists, and after we have ceased to be those things; before the Ego begins its work of attaching meaning to itself, clothing itself in identity, we simply *are*, full stop. Behind the machinations of our brilliant, undependable minds is an essence that is not conditional, a *being* that aging does not alter, to which nothing can be added, from which nothing is taken away. The more we become aware of this being, which is our Soul and the source of our strength, the less we will be prey to the illusion of meaninglessness. This is not an abstract concept; it is real as the breath moving in and out of your body, and real as the spirit that animates you. The greater your mindfulness, the more you will come to know this truth, and to rest in it when painful thoughts threaten to hide it from view.

As you will see, it is possible to experience this spaciousness even as painful events occur. As we try to practice mindfulness, we see that the Ego does not cease to exist—it simply ceases to tyrannize us or to offer the only version of experience available. Not being wholly dominated by our feelings, we are, in fact, able to feel them more deeply; knowing that a light exists, we may not be so afraid as before of peering into the darkness and discovering what it has to teach us. When we cease to resist our grief, for example, we learn that, painful though it may be, grief is an integral part of elder wisdom, a force that humbles and deepens our hearts, connects us to the grief of the world, and enables us to be of help. Grief need not paralyze the heart or become a garment for the Ego. I've met older people for whom grieving becomes an identity, the only role they feel fit to play. Grief has become a trap for them, which is why, if we are to learn from our darkness and contain it as a wounded elder bears his scars to heal and strengthen, we must be able to step outside our Egos, as Soul. Otherwise we are likely to be swept away by one or the other of grief's common fallouts, either closing our hearts in fear of the magnitude of our own feelings (and the feelings of those around us) and shrinking our lives to a "safe" zone that leaves us feeling half-alive; or becoming professional mourners, caught in the past with its loss and regret, unable to let go or to enjoy the present. As Saul Bellow wrote of such people in his great novel *Seize the Day*, "They're afraid that if they stop suffering, they will have nothing."

Depression and fear about aging both focus on losses. How much lack of Awareness we have when facing the losses determines how much we suffer. I recall being with my father at a stage of old age when he could not release the bitterness of his past failures. Dad found himself unable to speak of anything else. The mistakes he'd made, the roads he'd not taken, so colored his consciousness that soon the good he'd done in the world, and the many things that he had achieved, were obfuscated by his regrets until he felt that his entire life had been nothing but a failure. Fortunately, these stormy seas passed, and before he died, Dad came to see his life more clearly.

Depression

The sadness we often experience later in life may be just part of the Soul's evolution. Perhaps this depression is part of what Saint John calls the "dark night of the Soul," in which the Ego experiences a kind of death in order to allow the Soul to be born into its own full Awareness.

Although I was young, shortly before meeting my guru I underwent a depression that followed a similar course. I had begun to experience moments of Soul Awareness through the use of entheogens, but I was unable to sustain my own awakening and had nearly given up. I was feeling like a failure when I was brought to Maharajji. Shortly thereafter, I began to leave my former identity, my Richard Alpert-ness, behind, and to embark upon a journey of becoming Ram Dass, or Servant of God—a journey which continues to this day. Looking back it is clear to me that the despair I experienced was a prerequisite to what came next. The negative thing, the depression, pushed me to find something. The positive thing, the spiritual growth, pulled me out of the depression. I have witnessed similar cycles among friends on the path to consciousness, when they spiral into deep depressions that prove, in time, to be preparation for something else.

In this same way, I believe that the stripping-away of old habits, old self-image, old psychological crutches, physical strength, and worldly position, and the sense of depression these changes cause in the mind, may be seen as a necessary stage in our ripening and attaining wisdom.

There is a growing Awareness in the medical community

that a lot of what has been diagnosed and treated as depression among older people may instead be a natural process of reorientation. Whether we attribute it to cellular-biochemical mechanisms, or psychodynamics, or spiritual processes, there's a kind of drawing-inward that seems to be part of the process of aging. Not a paranoid drawing-inward; not being afraid of the world. Just a kind of deepening. I think it's probably the nearness of death that leads many people to want to reflect on what life is all about.

Age is an opportunity for considering questions like "What am I doing here? What has this all been about? Where am I in the flow of all this? How do I understand it all?" Many people deny themselves that rich experience; they label their yearning to reflect about their lives as something weird or wrong. They think they're supposed to stay busy all the time. But slowing down, drawing in, can open us to some of the most fruitful experiences of life, and some of the richest gifts that aging has to offer.

FACING FEAR

In order to approach dark mental states in this constructive way, however, we must be willing to face our fears. Just as children are often afraid of the dark, we may carry an aversion to night feelings into our old age. But just as children must learn to separate between what is real (the dark) and what is not (the bogeyman hiding under the bed), we must learn discernment and courage regarding our fears of aging. There are a number of bogeymen that accompany us into adulthood. The biggest one is this: "I'll be old and alone with no mind, and when I die I'll be alone, adrift, isolated in a cold, dark universe." The Ego is the only part of us that believes this.

As Gandhi said, "Fearlessness is the first prerequisite of a spiritual life." Fear means we're either worried about something that's already taken place, or anxious about things that haven't even happened. Bringing ourselves into the present moment can help us to loosen fear's stranglehold. In all spiritual practice, the strategy is the same: to identify the thing that frightens you and come as close to it as you can before you freak out. For example, if you are haunted by the fear of going blind, allow this thought and attendant images and feelings—the helplessness, the reliance on others, the darkness in your visual field— to arise without resistance. Watch how the fear manifests in your body, and guard against the desire to pull back. If this fear becomes too overwhelming to you, take a mental step back— our intention is not to create more drama, but to teach ourselves to hang out with our own fears or bogeymen, rather than to feed them by ignoring them. As we become more aware of the degree to which our fears are mind-states, rather than realities, we take our power back.

In a calm moment, allow yourself to consider the list of the most common fears and challenges facing us as we grow older, from the usual suspects listed above, to things like incontinence, abandonment, death. You may be surprised to realize that factors that frighten other people have no power over your mind, while less-common fears are dominant for you. Elisabeth Kübler-Ross tells the story of an old woman dying in a hospital who can't seem to let go of her body; against all odds, and to the distress of her doctors and family, this frail old lady kept hanging on. One day, Elisabeth was called in to talk to her— speaking candidly to the dying was rare in those days, sad to say—and asked the old woman what she was afraid of. "Being eaten by worms," she answered. The terror of being laid in the ground had been blocking this lady from letting go. At Elisabeth's urging, a document was signed by the lady's children in her presence, promising to have her body cremated. She died peacefully in her sleep the next day.

In the process of learning to become mindful, and to age in a conscious way, fearlessness is an essential ingredient. This fearlessness involves the willingness to tell the truth, to ourselves and others, and to confront the contents of our minds. We must be willing to look at everything—our own suffering as well as the suffering around us—without averting our gaze, and allow it to *be* in the present moment. Rather than closing ourselves to fear, we learn to open to it, to sit with it, allowing it to arise and pass in its own time. By simply looking, with no push or pull, mindfulness is strengthened. You will find that the moment you enter this witness state, the boundaries of the Ego are loosened, and fear begins to change. You will discover that the fearful thought you are looking at is quite different from the fear you've run away from; the minute you look at it and embrace it, the power is yours. I'm not suggesting that once this has happened, the same fear will not arise again, but you'll be seeing it from a different point of view. Rather than being some awful Goliath, your fears will become like little shmoos. Every time you notice a place in your mind where you sense denial, deepen your practice, and then come close to it. Invite it in for a cup of tea. "Fear of being paralyzed? Oh yeah. Haven't seen you for awhile. Why don't you come in and have some tea?" "Fear of dying? Oh, I see you every day. Well, come and sit down. Tell me what's been happening." Each time you can do this, you'll get a little closer to being able to look at it and say, "Ah, so."

4

THE BODY

IN

QUESTION

Well into my 60s, I denied that I was aging and ignored my body as much as possible. Besides my failed Superman routine that landed me onstage in Denver with a bloody leg, I had several other experiences that made this denial obvious to me, and I still have the scars to prove it. I boogie-boarded with twenty-year-olds in French Polynesia and wound up impaled on a coral reef. Golfing on a beautiful day with my youthful instructor, I imagined that I was her age and chased a ball down a muddy hill, ripping a rotator cuff in my shoulder. Another time, while helping a dear friend build his house in the mountains of New Mexico, I tried to match the strength of the young workers lifting adobe bricks on an assembly line and nearly collapsed.

I decided to start working out at Gold's Gym, and hired a personal trainer to help me build my muscles. This gym was renowned for its weight-lifting patrons, and everywhere around me, these huge, muscle-bound people were looking at themselves in mirrors, posing, admiring their bulging arms and chests. Soon I began to imitate them, sucking in my stomach and swaggering, but since I'm nearsighted without my glasses, I couldn't see myself in the mirror. I actually convinced myself that I was becoming one of them, until one day when I was doing my usual exercise, my trainer, with a concerned look on her face, asked me, "Are you all right?" I thought I was fine, she clearly did not. Sadly, I was forced to admit—again—that my body was not what I wished it would be.

56

This reminded me of a poem my father sent me long ago:

The gray in your hair doesn't make you old,
Nor the crow's feet under your eyes, I'm told.
But when your mind makes a contract your
body can't fill,
You're over the hill, friend, you're over the hill.

Over the hill or not, I had to admit that I wasn't the same.

It's ironic that I should be speaking on the subject of the body with anything like authority. The relationship I've had with my own body has been checkered at best. As a young man enduring the usual struggles with identity, emotions, and sexuality, I made an unconscious decision to subordinate my body. For many years, I was able to justify this denial by telling myself that I aspired to being a holy man, transcending the passions and pain of the flesh (though, of course, I never fully did). As I began to age, this denial seemed all the more justified; why in the world would I want to attach myself to a physical body that was obviously declining? Had I not spent my adult life emulating my beloved guru, whose body appeared to be of so little concern to him? Now was the chance to leave my body even farther behind and dwell in "higher consciousness."

I was deluding myself, of course, as I've learned since having this stroke and being forced to confront my body more directly than ever before. I've realized that I had been fleeing until then. I was not liberated, as I had imagined, but avoiding the limits of my own "incarnation." I can now see the difference between my fragmented mind-state and Maharajji's authentic bliss. Not only had his Soul been merged with the Absolute, but he was also deeply rooted in the body he seemed so oblivious to. There he sat on the ground with nothing between his skin and the dirt but an old blanket, at ease with his flesh and its mortal connection to all of nature around it. He saw his body for what it was, an aspect of God. He may have tended to downplay its importance, but he did not avoid it. At heart, I suspect he would have agreed with the Buddhist saying that the blessing of a human incarnation is beyond our ability to grasp, and that, once attained, it must be cherished.

Now that my stroke has made me more aware of my body, I finally feel qualified to say a few things about how we may age physically with grace, and use the changes in our bodies as a path of healing into God.

BODY IMAGE

Discontent with our changing body image as we age is a rich source of suffering for many people, and is intensified by advertisements and the pervasive notion that new things, and youthful people, are preferable to signs of wear and tear. This leads many old people to fight the aging process to an extent that makes their lives miserable. When dieting and exercise fail, we may seek the help of surgeons to alter how we look, often going to extraordinary lengths to hide our age. We need to examine our attitudes toward body image, the thoughts and feelings that arise at the images of ourselves in the mirror. Ask yourself: who am I now that my body is no longer what it was? What is the thing in me that has not changed, the "I" that is observing this process?

I'm not suggesting that we be Pollyana-ish; there's a sadness to seeing our bodies age that can't be denied, just as we experience loss at the flower losing its bloom. It's appropriate to look at the signs of age in our bodies, the varicose veins or balding heads, and sigh over the passing of time, or better yet, to chuckle. Many times catching sight of myself in a mirror, I've stopped and thought, "That can't be me!" The image of my bald head and sagging belly moves me to humor, not tears, so that I can say to myself, "Ah, so, even this."

This won't happen overnight. I had to go to the mirror a lot. I had to say to myself, "That's my bald head, that's my big belly, that's my sagging skin." I had to look at, accept, and develop tender compassion for every part of my body. I had to do this in order to find out who lived in this old apartment building. If I couldn't look at the apartment building, how would I ever find out if anyone was home? Try this sometime. There's so much freedom in it.

In India, they say that the snake doesn't rip off its old skin; in the proper time, the snake sheds its skin, like slipping out of a coat. In this same way, if we remain conscious of our tendency to cling to the past and bemoan the future, we can learn to accept our aging bodies with dignity, grace, and good humor, allowing our former appearance to slip off like the skin of the snake. But often this takes time.

I'll use my battle with being overweight as an example. For forty years, I fought with myself in the area of extra fat, swinging between diets and gluttony, caught in a no-win situation. Every milk shake and dessert brought guilt; every goody resisted brought feelings of deprivation. As I got older, the struggle to keep the pounds off became more and more difficult, but the habitual thought-pattern telling me that I was too fat, that I looked wrong when I let my body eat as it wished, and be bigger, was too deeply entrenched to be let go of easily.

Then I had an experience that changed this preoccupation. I was teaching for a week at a Jewish family summer camp, and late one Friday afternoon, I joined all the men for a *mikva*, or purifying bath, that involved immersing ourselves in a hot tub and then a swimming pool, en masse, naked. There were men and boys of all ages, and looking around, I suddenly saw myself reflected in many of the bodies around me, descended, as I was, from Eastern European peasant stock. I saw in that moment that the contours of my natural body, which I'd been fighting most of my life, were genetically ordained! I felt my compulsion to be thinner start to shift, and soon my body weight had stabilized at 215 pounds with no diet involved. Statistics say that this is a bit too high, but I ceased caring, and shed the attachment to a thinner-body image. I learned to appreciate my tummy rolls rather than fight them, which helped me relax—and helped me to prepare for my physical disability as well.

HOW TO USE LOW ENERGY

We can apply this same idea of acceptance to the issue of physical energy loss that comes with aging. Whether or not we undergo serious illness, the diminishment of physical energy as we age seems all but inevitable, and many people I've worked with report an increasing feeling of failure as they find themselves less able to perform effectively. They talk about taking twice as long to do half as much, and how this change in rhythm leaves them frustrated and depressed. Rather than accepting that "the old gray mare just ain't what she used to be," they whip themselves to little avail, pushing themselves beyond their limits or giving up entirely. We can, however, approach this issue more consciously. When you begin to feel tired—a little achy, a little weak, a tiny headache—notice the thoughts and feelings that accompany these things. Rather than fight your body's limits, try to stop and say, "Ah, less energy. New moment. Maybe I'll wait, or slow down, or stop." Allow yourself to be tired. Maybe you're already tired from reading this book, or from a long, stressful day. Close your eyes and feel into every inch of the fatigue.

I found an interesting device in Japan for examining my own reactions to changes in the feel of my body. It is called an *Urishimo Taro* kit, and consists of various weights and other paraphernalia to be attached to the body. These weights give one the experience of how it would feel to be old and frail, struggling to walk and do other common things, such as get up from the toilet. When I first put it on, I was struck by how my mind rebelled against the heavy physical sensation, so different from how I was used to feeling. I kept thinking, "How terrible this is!" rather than viewing the sensation as merely different. Eventually, as my mind began to settle down, I found myself able to adapt to the change in my physical state without resistance. Sometimes you've just got to go with the program.

One dynamic eighty-five-year-old complained to me, "I can't get anything done anymore. By the time I bathe and dress and take all my supplements and have breakfast, I'm too tired to do anything else!" Another friend, who's been a beehive of activity all her life, told me on the phone, "I don't know what's happening to me—I just want to lie around all the time. And I've got so many things to do!"

I said, "What have you got to do?"

She listed them. "Oh, so many things!"

I said, "Well, it sounds to me like one of the things you've got to do is to lie around. Would you add that to your list, and see where it fits into the priorities? Maybe you could say, 'I'll lie around first and then see if I have time for any of those other things.'" She called me later to say that she'd enjoyed her "creative lolling around" tremendously.

We should ask ourselves in moments of fatigue whether slowing down may not be a message to attend to the moment—to be with it . . . to taste it . . . to embrace it; a way of making us take time, finally, to tend to what's here now. Are these changes in energy a sign of how we could be evolving, quieting down, becoming more reflective? In India, this is the time when people look to give up their responsibilities and turn to the cultivation of the Soul. We've been busy—too busy—to do this in our youth. But the body's going. It's time to hear from the one who lives in the body, who lives in the personality that's been so busy achieving. By looking at our condition from the Soul's point of view, we can begin to flip our perspective and view the scene more creatively. "What's wrong with me?"—with its subsequent question of "How do I fix it?"—can become "What can this moment teach me? How can I use this slowness to tune in to the Soul?"

There are things we can do to prepare for the time when we'll have to slow down. I already mentioned one exercise in which we take the time to examine fatigue. There's another practice that's been used for thousands of years all over Asia. It's called walking meditation. I know. Walking. What's there to meditate on? Maybe nothing, maybe the entire universe. If we can't get ourselves to slow down in our daily routines, things like walking meditation can take us out of our daily routines, kidnap us, so that we can find the time to see what's in the moment. First, a warning. If you're not living in a spiritual community, or around a bunch of Buddhist monks and nuns, you may want to try this out alone or with a few simpatico types. Moving slowly, on purpose, can be a shock to the people around you, so dip in a bit at a time. In this practice, we clasp our hands lightly either in front of our waist or behind our back, focus our eyes on the ground three feet ahead of us, and slowly attend to each experience of walking. Watch for the slightest movement of the ankle, the heel, the bending of the toes. Feel the shift as the other foot flattens out to bear the weight of your body. Notice the intention to begin to place the moving foot onto the ground, first heel, then arch, then toes, the shift of weight again, as you intend to begin the process with the other foot. You'll become aware of your breathing, and aware of your thinking. Your mind will seem noisier. The noise was always there—you just never stopped to listen in. It's better to choose to hear the noise by slowing down voluntarily than to be stunned by what's inside later when you're forced to sit still. I have practiced this exercise for hundreds of hours over the years. Settling into this kind of pace can induce states of great inner peace. This will help you practice for when slowing down becomes a necessity, rather than a choice.

OUR BED OF WOESES

There's a lot, besides slowing down, to face about aging, and when I first tried, before I had my stroke, I had begun to compile a list of "top ten hits" of inevitable troubles. I used them as a contemplative exercise to pinpoint where my greatest fears lay. I would read the list very slowly, like a litany, pausing after each item to feel its effects on my mind and to open to the fear of it in my heart.

My list read something like this: *crippling arthritis, painful sciatica, chronic insomnia, constipation and its toxicity, high blood pressure, hardening of the arteries, metastatic cancer, congested lungs and shortness of breath, blindness, atrophying muscles, loss of bowel or bladder control, deafness, prostate cancer, interminable fatigue, chronic pain, osteoporosis, aneurysm, stroke.* Reading through the list, I was sensitive to which items hit me the hardest, and took additional time to reflect on the condition and allow it to enter my consciousness more deeply. Once I had done that, I began to investigate my thoughts and feelings surrounding the condition, and to discover whether the fear could be transformed by shifting my perspective.

For example, chronic insomnia was always a major thorn in this "bed of woeses." I've had sleep problems on and off during my life, and dread, as most insomniacs do, those hellish hours in the dark, tossing and turning. How many nights have I been tormented by the fear of not being able to sleep, the dread of being exhausted the next day, of not having enough energy to carry out my duties; worrying whether or not to drug myself, knowing I'll feel hung over the next day? I can't count the nights I've been so busy not sleeping that sleep couldn't come if it wanted to! And yet, when I reflect on insomnia, rather than being tyrannized by it, I'm able to see clearly how much of my suffering is self-imposed and avoidable. I can even see the time I spend not sleeping as an opportunity to do something else— meditating like a good yogi, for example, or watching my breath, listening to relaxing music, reading, or soaking in a bath. This is not to say I wouldn't *rather* be sleeping, but if I look at what is, I can alleviate some of my own suffering. Sounds simple. It is, and it isn't. If, as a lifelong insomniac, I were to make a deal with myself to spend those awake hours waking up, rather than becoming depressed, how different this condition might be. It reminds me of a namesake of mine in India, called Papa Ram Dass, who, when tortured all night by mosquitoes outdoors on the porch of the Ram temple, said, "Thank you Ram (God) for keeping me awake all night so that I could remember you."

Although we may never be that holy, we can begin to shift our thoughts, and our behavior that arises from physical troubles, in such a way as to ease our suffering rather than increase it. There are two things we can do to find our way out of the bed of woeses. The first is to notice and accept the suffering. When we become aware of what's in a moment, sometimes what's there isn't pleasant. Sink into every aspect of the moment and embrace the sleeplessness, the stomach pain, the headache, whatever's there. Then think about the neighbor you might know who's having a similar problem. Think about a family member or a friend; the people in your city, your state; the beings around the world and throughout the universe who might also be suffering. That's a big community you've just connected yourself to. They're human beings like you, wanting not to suffer. There's no reason why you should suffer, but no reason they should either. What would it be like if just by your suffering, all these millions of beings could be relieved of their suffering? Maybe thinking this wouldn't have any real effect on them, but on the other hand, maybe it would. And most important, you wouldn't feel alone in your own suffering anymore.

I'm not suggesting that we dwell on negative images, only recommending that we balance our habitual pattern of avoidance, fear, and dread with a measure of acceptance, so that when such conditions arise, we're able to say, "This, too," and welcome it as we have to welcome everything, rather than contract our minds and hearts. Each of us will find his or her own path to this acceptance—some through humor, others through sharing, still others through conscious spiritual practice—but whatever the means that allow us to live in our aging bodies with grace, rather than anger, morbidity, or denial, it is crucial that we find them.

In her diary, *At Eighty-two: A Journal*, the wonderful journal of solitary life in her elder years, the author May Sarton describes her inner life with unflinching honesty, and shows how her own practice—of gardening and recording her experience with a tape recorder—helped her to live with an ailing body. She wrote:

> "This extraordinary weather goes on. I have not
> been able to talk into this machine much lately be-
> cause I have been in so much pain, again with that

feeling of desperation. I do not know what to do with myself. But yesterday and today things were a little better. Today I had a normal (bowel) movement, which is such a grace that I really have to thank God. . . .

"The thing with pain is that you must go ahead and do what you want to do even if it hurts. That's how I managed to garden yesterday. Of course the satisfaction then outweighs the pain. Today I'm planning to put in three miserable looking iris that I ordered. . . .

"It's a grim day. I wish for the first time there were some way of leaving here forever. Then I would not have to watch the garden die. . . .

"I do feel depressed in spite of this nice find in the mail because I am again in trouble with my digestion. I thought I had found a way to solve the problem. I am in a lot of pain today and yesterday. I do not see a way out. . . .

"So it's a difficult situation. I must say I went to bed last night in a traumatized state because of the perilousness of life on all sides, knowing that any moment something frightful may happen."

Sarton isn't dressing up her feelings, but even in her worst despair, we see her keenly observing the whole process. There's a thread of witness there, and while her practice of watching her own experience does not remove her physical suffering, it allows her an outlet for conditions that otherwise might have left her defeated; a resting place in which to be truthful, and create something beautiful (a book, a garden) from her pain.

Following my stroke, I started to collect different methods of treatment—traditional Western ones, alternative ones, spiritual ones. Someone would call or write to tell me about this therapy or that medicine, and I would discuss them with my doctors and friends. Some of the recommendations I would follow, some not. One friend suggested a treatment which increased oxygen levels in the brain. I traveled to Beverly Hills for this particular one. When you walked into the room, it was filled with tanks that looked like suspended animation tanks from the film *2001: A Space Odyssey*. Each patient was meant to climb into one of these pressurized oxygen tubes and hang out for an hour. I'd meditate or listen to music. I had forty treatments. We patients were a varied group—everything from stroke patients like me, to deep-sea divers recovering from the bends, to people speeding their healing from plastic surgery. It was quite the Beverly Hills scene.

My own healing has flowed from many, many sources: my guru, my use of medical marijuana, the help of several shamans, acupuncture treatments, biofeedback, an experimental drug called acetylcholine, pills, pills, and more pills, aquatherapy, physical therapy, Feldenkrais, speech therapy, and—most of all—love from so many people . . . *so* many people!

I went through a process of both healing and curing. While cures aim at returning our bodies to what they were in the past, healing uses what is present to move us more deeply to Soul Awareness, and in some cases, physical "improvement." As I've said, although I have not been cured of the effects of my stroke, I have certainly undergone profound healings of mind and heart that have made these past two years among the happiest of my life. To the Ego this seems impossible; a rationalization of pain, a coping mechanism, or a delusion, but the Ego is only one facet of who we are. The body and its aging journey can be viewed from a larger perspective. When we look at the shifts in our physical state from a Soul perspective, the difference is remarkable: instead of bemoaning the loss of who we were, we marvel at who we are becoming. If we know that we are more than the body, we're free to relate to it less fearfully, with mercy, instead of resentment, toward its aches and pains. Seeing the body as a part of nature, we do not fear the signs of death in quite the same way as before. We may even learn to love our bodies, and to appreciate their different beauty, as they change from young to old.

This isn't easy. Whether we wish to acknowledge it or not, our fear of the body as it ages is simply a mask for the fear of death, which I will go into more deeply in Chapter Seven. For now, we must be perfectly clear that the aversion we feel toward our skin as it wrinkles, our muscles as they sag, our bodies as they "fail" us in age, stems from the Ego's knee-jerk aversion to any reminders of death. The body is the house of death, and in order to live with it through its decline, it will help to be mindful of this connection. The discomfort felt inside the body as it hits sixty, seventy, or eighty, is not merely esthetic or a matter of function: in facing the body we face the evidence of death's slow or quickening approach, and to fear, reject, or ignore our bodies is not very different from killing the messenger of unwanted news to the king, the Ego, who rejects the notion of the body's own death.

On a less-abstract level, many of us face real physical challenges that trouble us, and the prospect of others to come. Most of us try not to think about these things at all, if we can avoid it—and when we're forced by circumstance to confront them, we feel the tightening in our stomachs, the contraction in our hearts, and the anxiety coursing through us. Avoidance of our fears only feeds them. It is useful to be honest with ourselves about the aspects of our bodies that frighten us as we age.

WORKING WITH PAIN

As I've learned from personal experience, pain is a formidable opponent. When I first had my stroke, the doctors were not able to give me enough pills to deaden the pain of my body as it tightened and became paralyzed. Since then, the pain has become more manageable, but still it is an ongoing effort to remain mindful of the physical sensations rather than allowing the fear of those sensations to dominate my consciousness. I've learned that you can't work with pain when you are stuck in fear and aversion. At the same time, if I know that I am more than this body, I can shift to the Soul perspective. It becomes a refuge—not for hiding, but for learning to separate the fear of pain from the actual sensation.

Though this practice has become an ongoing necessity for me, most of us have had some experience of intense physical discomfort to help us identify with the extreme suffering that can come in older age. One of mine came many years ago during an acute case of hepatitis. I was in a hotel room far up in the Himalayas, with no electricity, no automobile, and nowhere to go. I didn't know what was happening to me; the pain in my abdomen was excruciating, and I found myself writhing on the floor under the bed. In the first hours my mind was racing: "Get a doctor! Get medicine!" On one level, I was in a total panic. At the same time, I was chanting "Ram, Ram, Ram," the name of God. Once I surrendered to the fact that I could do nothing but the prayerful repetition of the name of God, the most extraordinary shift occurred. I began to be fascinated by what was happening—I would almost say, to enjoy what was happening to me, strange as this sounds to the rational mind. Though the pain was terrible, not identifying completely with the fear allowed me to survive the ordeal.

Surrendering to pain is just like surrendering to fatigue. It's frightening to think about not fighting pain, as though we'll lose something, or be killed by it if we open up to it. But the truth is that nothing will happen to us. Pain can't hurt us, but the fear of pain can. It can make us run around doing all kinds of crazy things, snapping at those closest to us or avoiding a much-needed trip to the doctor to find out what's causing the pain. We've all been there. The next time you feel pain, try learning to welcome it. It's there, as a signal from the body to attend, so you might as well invite it in. Just like with insomnia, or fatigue, you could try this with the flu. Feel the heat of your skin and the aches from the fever. Sink into them. Relax when you dive into the stuffed sinus passages. Not only will you suffer less from the illness, you'll be taking the time you need to rest. And if you can, think of all the other beings throughout the universe who might be suffering from the same thing. Send them your caring and wishes for a speedy recovery.

You will find that each time you're able to welcome your own pain, you'll also be welcoming the Soul, and the Soul is what can defeat the fear and suffering of pain. If you can learn to relax into the experience, and not push the sensations away, you will see your own suffering start to change. Stephen and Ondrea Levine have done a lot of important work in developing meditations for embracing pain, rather than treating it as an enemy. They've shown how our reflexive response to armor ourselves against painful sensation, building a wall between it and us, only exacerbates the pain by creating more fear: that if we let down our barriers, we'll hurt more. Of course, it is best to begin this practice with minor complaints so that if something serious should occur, you have sufficient presence of mind to meet it with experience.

Regardless of the severity of our condition, we have a choice in how we relate to it. I see this every day of my life. A friend of mine who's been stricken by severe arthritis is spending a great deal of mental energy holding onto the image of himself as he was before, and keeping himself in a near-constant state of anxiety. He's afraid of the arthritis getting worse, worries about where it will flare up next, and clings to regrets about the ways his life has changed. While I certainly understand his reaction, I also see how his Ego is sabotaging any hopes of peace with what is. Were he to practice viewing his arthritis from the Soul level, the dialogue he maintains with himself might change from panic, despair, and rage, to something like this: "I see the arthritis. I'll go to the doctors to see if there's anything they can do to help get me free of it, but in the meantime I'll give up the model of being somebody without arthritis. I will say 'hello' to the knee that gives out when I climb two stairs, and the fingers that can't grip the lid of a jar."

This is precisely what another friend, the theologian Huston Smith, has managed to do. When Huston, who's close to 80, came down with a painful case of facial shingles, I called to ask him how he was, expecting a factual medical update. Instead, he said to me, "Apparently somebody up there has decided to offer me another teaching."

THE MIRROR OF SUFFERING

Over the years, I've found great benefit for my heart in hanging out with people—young and old—who have major disabilities, and I realize now how this has helped me on my own journey of conscious aging. Whether their bodies have been incapacitated by physical trauma, disease, or old age makes little difference, since the results are the same. I consider them among my most cherished teachers.

Kelly was one such friend for me. When Kelly was ten, he was hit on the head with a baseball, and when fluid and pressure built up inside his skull, the hospital emergency room misdiagnosed the situation—twice. This resulted in Kelly's becoming a quadriplegic, requiring round-the-clock care. When we met, Kelly was in his late 20s, and despite his severe limitations, he had attended college and was living a rich life, full of interests and loving friends. He had come to one of my lectures, and his presence there in the gurney, with his drooping head and drooling mouth, drew me to him. Although he couldn't speak, he could spell out his thoughts on an alphabet board with an assistant's help. Kelly "told" me via this board that he was having difficulty with his anger and frustration, and that he wanted my help. This began a friendship that lasted eight years, until his death.

At first, I had difficulty spending time with Kelly. In fact, it took me six months of twice-a-week visits before I was able to quiet down enough inside to sit next to his grotesquely deformed body without an intense emotional reaction. Then I finally met Kelly the Soul, who existed in this body, but was not trapped in *identification* with that form. Once this shift had occurred for me, it was smooth sailing between us. Our Souls were able to meet in the midst of this physical suffering and find appreciation together.

Once, Kelly asked to be allowed to introduce me at a lecture I was giving to a large conference of professional healers. I was uneasy at first, wondering what would happen, but I finally agreed. When Kelly was wheeled out onto the stage, there was a stunned, uneasy silence as the audience reacted to Kelly's circumstance. Then with the help of an assistant, he spelled out his introduction letter by letter on the board. His assistant read the message. "R. D. (Kelly's name for me) says we are not our bodies. Amen." The audience gave him a standing ovation.

Kelly helped me get free of my own reactivity to such severely disabling conditions, and I helped him get free of his anger. I discovered that inside his body was a Soul that was ripe to be free after years of trauma. Recently I had another such opportunity, with a fellow in his mid-thirties who was in the final stages of ALS, also known as Lou Gehrig's disease. When we met, he had no voluntary control over any part of his body except his facial muscles. He communicated by code, pursing his lips for a dot and raising his eyebrows for a dash. The first time I sat by his bedside and we "talked," I was aware—as I had been at first with Kelly—of an intense feeling of claustrophobia inside myself that was awakened by empathy. I had difficulty not identifying with him, living inside that crippled body—just as people must have had at times now with me—but as I quieted down and sat there, my hand resting in his hand, we fell into a deep silence. The anxiety subsided in me and I was bathed in a radiance of peace. When I opened my eyes, he spelled out with his face the words, "Much light, much peace." Neither of us was trapped at that moment.

While my momentary experiences of empathy were certainly not the same as being inside such a body day after day, they showed me the possibility that awakening to Soul identification can make even such an extreme life scenario rich in its moment-by-moment beauty. When we see someone who has been able to embrace a really profound change in physical circumstances, it rekindles our appreciation for the resilience of the human spirit. What's more, learning to dis-identify myself with Kelly's difficulties with his body, to be mindful of his suffering without taking it on, is similar to the challenges we face with our own bodies, learning to be mindful of our physical state, and to be compassionate toward it. If we can't find compassion for ourselves, we'll never find it for anyone else.

It is helpful to know, as we age, how we might wish to respond should we receive a diagnosis of a life-threatening disease. Many older people I've spoken to harbor an almost superstitious aversion to thinking about such matters, but now that we're learning about conscious aging, we're free to let such superstitions go. Disease is a simple fact of life and the older we get, the more likely we are to become ill with something or other. Our challenge now, as conscious beings, is how to meet these changes wisely. We need to plan for how we'll deal with a serious illness, because sooner or later it will happen to most of us.

About ten years ago, the MacArthur Foundation gave one of its "genius awards" to a wonderful fellow named Michael Lerner, who works with people diagnosed with cancer. His description of what he would do if faced with a cancer diagnosis seems to me extremely helpful:

> "I would pay a great deal of attention to the inner healing process that I hoped a cancer diagnosis would trigger in me. I would give careful thought to the meaning of my life, what I had to let go of and what I wanted to keep.

> "I would give careful thought to choosing a mainstream oncologist. I wouldn't need someone with wonderful empathic skills because I have other people to provide that. But I would want a doctor who is basically kind, is on top of the medical literature regarding my disease, takes the time to answer my questions, understands that I want to be deeply involved in treatment decisions, supports my use of complementary therapies, and sticks with me medically and emotionally if I were facing death.

"I would use conventional therapies that offered a real chance for recovery, but I would probably not use experimental therapies or therapies with a low probability of success that were highly toxic or compromised my capacity to live and die as I choose.

"I would use complementary therapies. I would look for a good support group and a psychotherapist experienced in working with people with cancer. I've been a vegetarian for many years but I would look for ways to enhance my nutrition. I would meditate and practice yoga more often, and spend more time in nature, taking walks in the woods, by the ocean, and in the mountains.

"I would definitely use traditional Chinese medicine, both herbs and acupuncture.

"I would strive for life and recovery, with every possible tool and resource I could find. But I would also work to face death in a way that deepened my growth and led to some resolution.

"I would spend time with people I value, and with books, writing, music, and God. I would do everything that I could do that I didn't want to leave undone. I would not waste time with old obligations, though I would try to extricate myself from them decently.

"I would try to live my own life in my own way. I would try to accept the pain and sorrow inherent in my situation, but I would look searchingly for the beauty, wisdom, and the joy.'"

Although Michael does not use the word Soul, or Witness, his balanced view reflects a way of meeting disease as consciously and holistically as possible. Though he would utilize

Western medicine, he would complement allopathic treatment with "alternative" methods; though he would strive to cure his body, he would not neglect the healing of his Soul through art, prayer, and relationship. This integrative relationship to our bodies and their diseases reflects the kind of multi-level Awareness we need to cultivate in order to age more consciously. We can give our physical selves their proper care and respect without allowing their impermanent nature to tyrannize our entire being. Most of us have met older people who reduce themselves to the sum of their physical ailments, fears, or complaints. I once saw several old people sitting on a park bench in Florida talking about their ailments: "Oh, my gallbladder came out, oh, my liver is bad, oh, my kidneys don't work, my intestines hurt, my heart's been operated on." This is "the organ recital." This kind of complaining seems to happen for two reasons: first, having retired from the workplace, with children grown, and not much to do, they become focused primarily on their bodies; and secondly, they are drawn to the topic by the increase in the frequency of physical ailments they encounter. While we certainly sympathize with this common predicament, it is important to be on the lookout for this tendency toward over-identification with ailing bodies, the too-inviting cushion of our "bed of woeses."

This trap is often set, unconsciously, by those around us, whose sympathy can become imprisoning for the attention-seeking Ego. Since I had my stroke, it has been an ongoing practice to stay free of other people's pity, and not to be trapped into fulfilling the role that some have projected onto me as invalid, victim, hero. On a far less serious level, I learned this lesson a few years ago when I went into the hospital for minor surgery. No sooner had friends heard the S-word than they started showering me with cards and flowers, chicken soup, all the signs and proofs of concern. Because of a minor medical procedure, I was being showered with gifts, and with warnings: "Be careful," "Don't do this or that," "Let me know if you need anything," "Are you *sure* you're all right?" I saw then, and have learned ever since, that while others mean well by these shows of concern, they can easily seduce the Ego into the role of sick person—or sick body—and keep us stuck where we don't belong.

In order to get out of these traps, which can plunge us into self-pity, I have tried to focus on the compassionate aspects of the various meditations suggested in this chapter. With my heart open, I take the time to empathize for a moment with those who suffer the way I do. I believe that our thoughts have spiritual power, and with this intention in mind, I send a silent message to my fellows: "Hey, you are not alone. The rest of us are right here with you."

Naturally, as our bodies change, so do our behaviors and the ways we relate to the society around us. As these relationships change, it is important to examine how our roles shift—in our families, our communities, and the world in general. We will examine this in our next chapter.

5

SHIFTING
ROLES

Age is opportunity no less
Than youth itself, though in another dress,
And as the evening twilight fades away
The sky is filled with stars invisible by day.

—LONGFELLOW

There is no right or wrong way of growing old. A great source of suffering in our culture, and one which hounds many people as they age, is that if they could just figure out how to do things *right*, there would be no suffering in age. If they could just learn to *succeed* in aging correctly, as they've struggled to succeed in marriage, parenthood, business, and other areas of their lives, age would cease to bring challenges they didn't quite know how to face. But when it comes to how we choose to live, creating our lives and the roles we play as we move along in years, the rigid notion of right and wrong, and of success in general, should be irrelevant to how we make our decisions. We're finally free to make "mistakes," follow our hunches, experiment boldly, or *do nothing at all*, as age liberates us from our old roles and offers us the chance to seize an authentic way of being.

The wisdom of age is more a matter of being than of role playing. It's not a matter of trying to fulfill a social role; it's a matter of becoming wisdom itself. Yes, it is a role for the Ego to play, but here we need a deeper understanding of the Ego. The Ego is the program that runs personality, the body, and interactions with others on the physical plane. It can be a very useful tool. The Ego only becomes destructive when a person identifies the Ego as her or his whole being. That brings tremendous suffering, because the Ego is full of desires the fulfillment of which will never bring lasting happiness. Such a person becomes trapped in time and desires. If you take the perspective of the Ego, then there is suffering as the Ego struggles to preserve its identity in the face of the Soul's desire to merge with God. I tried to go the renunciate's way, to forget the needs of the body in order to avoid the suffering of the Ego. But the Soul depends on the Ego's drama for its teachings. We have to be in the world to learn from it.

The Buddha learned this lesson on his path to enlightenment. He heard about a bunch of great yogis sitting in meditation day and night and eating no more than a grain of rice every day. He did this for awhile until he realized he was assaulting the very vehicle that allowed him to travel a spiritual path. When he decided to travel the middle way—not indulging himself, but not remaining an ascetic—a lot of followers left him. But it was his appreciation of reality—the good and the bad—that led to his own enlightenment.

It took me a long time to understand that the renunciate path I learned in India just didn't work for me. Ultimately, I had to learn my Soul lessons through karma-yoga, which is using everything in life as the spiritual path. It is only by living with a fully functional Ego that the Soul has a chance to collect the data it needs to learn. The body, Ego, and Soul are in an interdependent relationship. Honor the body as a precious temple. Honor your Ego as the conduit of learning for the Soul.

ALL THE WORLD'S A STAGE

One of the best parts of aging is entering the "don't know," learning to be someone who can rest comfortably in uncertainty. There are as many ways of embodying wisdom as there are people on this earth. Each of us brings his or her own particular temperament and biography to the project of his or her own conscious aging. Just as there is no right or wrong way of doing this, there is no optimal picture of how you will look, or live, or love, as you wake up in this new phase of being. You will simply be more who you've always been.

Before going further, let's pause a moment to contemplate what we mean by "playing a role" and why it is that we're trained to do it. Only then can we properly understand how we may go about freeing ourselves.

The Ego is an actor by trade. As children learning to define this amorphous thing that we call our "selves," and to locate our place in the world, we are taught to draw boundaries across reality, gradually narrowing what we call "me" to the narrow confines of the Ego. Once "separated" from the world "out there," and all the other people in it, we proceed to construct an identity based on our likes and dislikes, the lessons we're taught, the requirements of environment, our physical attributes, inherited traits, and experiences, as well as the myriad other conditions that determine our material (and mental) existence. In its process of formation, the bulk of which takes place during the first seven years of life, the Ego can be compared to an actor preparing for the stage. It selects its costumes, learns its lines, its timing, its gestures, its way of movement, even the choices of roles it may play when it leaves the dressing room and stands before an audience of other Egos across the footlights. Unlike an actor, however, who realizes that he or she is onstage playing a role, we tend to forget who we really are once we've taken the stage, like the mime whose mask becomes stuck to his face, hiding the true face underneath.

One of the reasons that old age is so disconcerting to many people is that they feel as if they're stripped of their roles. As we enter old age and face physical frailty, the departure of children, retirement, and the deaths of loved ones, we see the lights fading, the audience dwindles, and we are overwhelmed by a loss of purpose, and by the fear of not knowing how to behave or where we now fit in this play. The Ego, whose very sustenance has been the roles it played in the public eye, becomes irate, despairing, or numb, in the face of its own obsolescence. It may harken back to roles in its past to assert itself, but these strategies bring only more suffering as the Ego fights a losing battle.

As we learn to distinguish between our Egos—marked by our mind and thoughts—and the witness Soul—who's not subject to them—we begin to see the opportunity that aging offers. We begin to separate who we are from the roles that we play, and to recognize *why* the Ego clings as it does to behaviors and images that no longer suit us. Stripped of its roles, the Ego is revealed as fiction. But for the person without a spiritual context, this is pure tragedy, for seekers of truth who are aware of the Soul, it is only the beginning.

Rather than wonder what new "role" we can invent for ourselves in the world then, the question that concerns us might be better put this way: How can we, as aging people, make our wisdom felt in the world? By embodying wisdom. We can find a happy balance between participation and retreat, remembering that while it is our duty to be of service if possible, it is also important that we prepare for our own journeys into death, through contemplation, quiet time, and deepening knowledge of ourselves.

BEING VERSUS DOING

As we age, we become aware of the degree to which we've confused who we are with what we do. As the Ego-actor identifies itself with the various roles it plays throughout our lives, it begins to derive its sense of self-worth from what it accomplishes in the world. In the materialistic culture that has risen up after the Industrial Revolution, this emphasis on productivity is especially keen. Along with that comes a fear of retirement. It is almost as if we believe that once we stop producing and achieving, we cease to have value.

When I was a little boy, my mother used to give me little gold stars on the refrigerator for my achievements, teaching me that the more stars I earned, the worthier I was. Most of us have been raised with similar messages which we carry with us throughout our lifetimes. Is it any surprise, then, that we feel lost and purposeless when, with age, our culture takes away our opportunities for achievement? Most people believe that what they do is who they are, rather than recognize that what we do is only part of who we are. As our lives change, and the opportunities for achievement-reinforcement diminish, we may experience boredom, depression, despair, and disempowerment. We're haunted by a sense that the ways we'd like to spend our time—sitting under a tree, for instance, or listening quietly to music—are trivial, and somehow wrong. Aware of how addicted we are to external reinforcement assuring us that we're "good enough," we're uneasy in retirement from achieving.

Uncomfortable as this predicament is, it provides an ideal opportunity for freeing ourselves from an outdated illusion. As many women who've gone through the painful phase known as "empty nest syndrome" have described, it is precisely the loss of their long-held parental role, difficult as that loss and the empty space it creates are, which invites them to move forward into a new way of life. The Ego loses the productive roles which gave it a sense of identity and worth. That creates suffering for the Ego. When you make the Ego uncomfortable, that's your chance to learn on a Soul level. When you take the identification with a role away, you stop feeding the Ego its usual fare.

By learning to rest in our Soul identity, we free ourselves and those around us from the old-young dichotomy. If I walk into a doctor's office and see the man in the white coat as a fellow Soul, I free myself from being the ignorant one in the presence of an expert. Whether the doctor sees me as a fellow being or as Patient #462 as we dance through our doctor-patient choreography depends on how caught he is in his role; the doctor's perception is the doctor's problem, not mine.

I experienced this flexibility in roles when I had to go to the hospital for shoulder surgery. When I walked through the doors of the hospital, I was not only "geriatric," but also "patient." The woman at the admissions desk recognized me, and after we'd talked for a few moments she said, "I know you work with death and dying, and I wonder if you'd spend a moment with my associate here, because she just lost her husband."

I asked her friend, "When did your husband die?"

"Five months ago," she said.

I asked, "Well, how's it going?" and we started talking about the roller coaster of grief, the ups and downs, and about how love transcends death. Through our simple conversation we opened to each other, meeting as Souls appreciating the horrible beauty of her situation. And it took us all of about five minutes. When I left that room, she and I both felt renewed.

THE MYSTERY OF SEX

In my groups on aging, I have found it difficult to speak about the dwindling of sexual interest. It is not a message that many people want to take in, and they often greet my confession with embarrassment or misunderstanding, so I tell them this story: An older man is walking down the street one afternoon when he hears a voice saying, "Pssst—could ya help me out?" He looks around, but there's nobody there. He starts to walk on, and again he hears, "Pssst—could ya help me out?" Once again he stops and looks around, and again, there's nobody to be seen. But this time he looks more carefully, and happens to glance down at the sidewalk, where he sees a huge frog. Though he's a little embarrassed to be talking to a frog, he asks: "Did you speak to me?"

Much to the man's surprise, the frog answers: "Yes, indeed. Could ya help me out?"

The man is intrigued and asks, "Well, what do you want?"

The frog replies, "Well, I'm under a curse. If you would kiss me, I would be freed of the curse, and I would turn into a beautiful woman, who would love you and serve you. I would care for you, warm your bed, and make you so happy!"

The man stands there for a moment, reflecting, and then picks up the frog, puts it into his pocket, and walks on. After a few minutes the frog says, "Hey! You forgot to kiss me."

And the man says, "You know, at my age, I think it might be more interesting to have a talking frog."

The story helps us see the humor in our predicament. Aging is what it is: as our bodies change, our sexual roles change or fall away. Just as our sexual roles changed once before, at puberty, we feel ourselves undergoing a major shift in desire and self-image that may leave us wondering who we are without our previous compulsion. As our physical passions cool, we may feel enormous loss and confusion over our shifting relationships. Just as our interest in trading baseball cards with buddies and sharing dolls with girlfriends once gave way to romantic dating, we may find ourselves attracted to different sorts of people for quite different reasons.

The shift from sex object to "sex optional" is fascinating for the Ego, as I can report from personal experience. Well into my 50s, I spent a great deal of energy on my sexual appetites, and on appearing sexually attractive to those around me. The older I became, however, the less power that sexual currency seemed to wield. People seemed to treat me differently—they treated me with less desire but more respect, and at first this shift aroused ambivalent feelings. I couldn't help feeling betrayed by my years, as if I'd been robbed of something I hadn't enjoyed sufficiently when I'd had the chance. I felt remorse for missed opportunities, and troubled myself with fantasies of all the pleasure that might have been, but hadn't, because of my psychological makeup. These regrets lasted for a number of years before I was able to settle down and relinquish the self-pity of the past. When this finally happened, I was amazed by how much more time and attention I had for other things in my life when the trumpets of sexual desire quieted down. Of course it's true that older people don't have to give up their sexual pleasures, and that many people enjoy rich sex lives well into their seventies and eighties. However, when the appetites fall away, it can also be a blessing.

At one of Omega's conscious aging conferences, a man walked up to me after my lecture and blurted out very proudly, "I'm seventy-six, and I get an erection every morning." Now I don't doubt this man's pronouncement; there are yogis in India who live well into their hundreds and have erections every day. I don't think there's any time limit, if you bring your will and concentration to the use of your *prana*, or life energy. Yogis who cultivate such powers can use them to be sexually active at any stage. One old yogi I saw could even lift a bag of cement with his erect penis. (Don't try this at home!) But these are not yogic practices to which I am particularly drawn.

Perhaps the hidden truth of the matter is that, just as most of us cease collecting baseball cards when we reach puberty, there's no need to keep collecting sexual experiences into our older age unless these relationships enrich us. Perhaps we don't have to feel diminished as our sexual roles weaken—to feel that we've failed, for example, if as men we experience impotence, or as women the cessation of desire—but instead can view this change as an opportunity to turn our attention to the new phases of our curriculum, and to new forms of intimacy.

This decrease in sexual interest, from inside and out, is equally confusing to women as to men. Thanks to advances in technology, women can now expect to live a third of their lives after menopause, and many women I've spoken to report confusion, if not distress, over how the culture views them once their roles—as sex object, wife, or mother—are taken away. As one woman said to me, "I'll walk down the street, and nobody even sees me. I feel like I don't exist any more." Deprived of this status, and no longer the focal point of a family, many women find it difficult to find a new role for themselves. How different this is from societies equipped with rituals to honor the later stages of life! In the Jewish community, for example, celebrations are traditionally held for a woman when her last child gets married, initiating her into cronehood. Even joining AARP at fifty is becoming a ritual to invite us through the door into a new stage of life.

THE MYTH OF THE INDIVIDUAL

We come to this challenge at a particularly confusing time. Our culture has little patience for wise elders, crones, or passers-on of the lineage. Fortunately, as the baby-boom generation enters the ranks of the elderly, we will have the opportunity to transform this situation. Many have been raised in a consciousness-seeking era and will refuse to be viewed as irrelevant. It wasn't so very long ago that elders had a role to play in our households. Due to economic necessity and social structures, individuals acknowledged that they were part of a complex network of natural and social systems: part of a family, part of a neighborhood, part of a nation-state, part of a biotic community, and so on. The importance of the individual was twofold, as both a separate entity and a part of a greater system.

Unfortunately, this interdependent vision has dwindled as the cult of individualism has grown stronger in the past fifty years. As a culture, we have moved away from households where children lived with parents and grandparents, uncles and aunts—where older people had a significant role to play in daily life—to the single-family dwelling (and often to the single-parent home). This fragmentation has left a majority of our elderly without a context in which to feel significant, and many old people feel that without a place in a connecting system, their lives have no meaning.

Besides feeling alienated from the structures of family and community, we also suffer the severing of our connection to the natural world, our biotic community. This deprives us of a feeling of appropriateness regarding the cycles of our lives and the naturalness of the aging process. Living in urban or suburban areas, surrounded by the projections of the human mind, we are rarely able to experience, in our blood and our being, the cycle of birth, aging, and death.

I became intensely aware of the degree to which this loss of place, in nature and family, has affected our aging population during an interview I conducted several years ago with Oren Lyon, the head of the Onondaga tribe in New York State. Oren had been an advertising executive in New York as a young man, but returned to his Native American roots in later years. In his tradition, an individual's identity was part of a seven-generation line, the three preceding and three after, but as Oren spoke to me, I could feel his despair. His grandchildren weren't listening, he told me.

As a child of the immigrant movement, I found it hard to grasp this concept of reliance on ancestors and future generations to provide one's identity. Having come to the New World full of dreams and expectations, my forebears were eager to let go of the past and to embrace the future. While this forward-looking philosophy has engendered a great deal of progress, I began to see how it had also deprived the aging children of immigrant parents of their roots, and of their historical sense of belonging.

A while back, I took part in running what's called an Elder Circle. The oldest people in the group sat in a circle, and the younger people sat around them. We had a talking stick, from the Native American tradition, and anybody from the inner circle who wanted to could take the talking stick, and share their wisdom with the rest of the group. It was interesting to hear how many of the people in the inner circle said, "This is a role I'm totally unfamiliar with, because nobody's ever asked me to be wise before." So many of them flowered in the richness of that opportunity to share their wisdom.

Because it does not know what to do with older people, our society has become impoverished of precisely those qualities its elders could offer. Unfortunately, most elders don't know, themselves, what it is they have to offer. And remember that young people won't be coming to our doors saying, "Hey, old folks, you've got something we want. We need your wisdom and perspective." It is only as we become more conscious, as a culture, that we will become more aware of our elder-gifts and how they might be shared. Aging consciously, we will naturally begin to manifest those qualities that our society needs in order to survive—qualities like sustainability, justice, patience, and reflection. These are qualities that can only come from the space of dispassionate perceptual Awareness which age invites us to explore.

CONSCIOUS CONNECTIONS

As our roles shift in older age, so does our sense of community, and feelings of isolation often accompany elder life. When I spoke about this to Thich Nhat Hanh, a Vietnamese Zen Master, he said that in spite of the information age and advances in technology, which allow us to communicate with each other so rapidly, "one human being can't *be with* another human being [through technology]. A father can't be with a son, a mother with a daughter, a father with a daughter, a friend with a friend." It's harder and harder for human beings to be together, even though they can transmit information to more and more people all the time.

Although relationships change in all stages of life, it often seems harder to find new connections to replace the ones we lose as we age. This effort to stave off loneliness and to replace missing connections can sometimes take extreme forms, as in a case I read about in which a Japanese man hired a surrogate couple with a baby to visit his elderly parents because he didn't have the time. The old people spent the day pretending that these strangers were their actual family, talking about their "grandchild's" health, how much the baby had grown, and so on. Before the surrogate couple left, kisses were exchanged and promises to visit again soon, and they were paid by the son the equivalent of $1,150 for their time and thespian abilities.

Caring for someone else is one way to combat loneliness. In response to this need, some older people have taken it upon themselves to be of service. Laura Huxley created Project Caress, a public space located in a shopping center where mothers and fathers can leave their babies while they shop. With a registered child-care professional in attendance, older people volunteer to come in to hold and cuddle the babies. The babies and the elders alike benefit from the contact. Although we may yearn to be quieter as we age, human beings have an inborn need for social contact that must be honored if we are not to suffer, and part of our conscious-aging curriculum must include finding ways to satisfy this yearning. We long to reassure ourselves that other hearts exist; to affirm our own existence through the presence of others. An older couple I know—he's a psychiatrist, she's a meditation teacher—have a big, beautiful home, where they raised a large family. After the children moved away and started families of their own, my friends were left rattling around in their big house, until one day they said, "This is a waste! Here we are in this wonderful house—why don't we fix up the basement and move down there, and give one of our kids and his family the upper floor?" Their son and his family really benefitted by having the house, and my friends enjoyed the cross-generational companionship.

Through a strange set of circumstances, another friend of mine found herself starting a family she never intended to have. At the age of 69, she became the sole caregiver for a six-year-old child. Here was a woman traveling the world to give seminars, writing books, being an intellectual, who suddenly had her life "interrupted" by a child she could not turn away. For the first few years, she bemoaned her fate, but slowly this changed, and she and the child are doing fine. She even admits that her life is better for this unexpected change of plan.

Even though, as Thich Nhat Hanh reminded us, we cannot *be* together through technology, cyberspace can afford us a different way of maintaining connection in older age. No longer bounded by geography, we can meet in the brave new world of the Internet and spend time as companions in virtual reality. A woman speaking on National Public Radio recently reported how she'd used her computer and her Internet contacts with people all around the country to get through her depression and loneliness after the death of her husband. A year later, she's become the one who is counseling and supporting other recent widows in a chat group on the Web. A friend of mine who is approaching seventy is teaching her still older next-door neighbor, a shut-in, how to surf the Internet. My friend, who loves gardens, shares (among other things) a spirited international Internet chat group on gardening. I foresee that computers will play an increasingly important role in engaging elders like me in educational and social participation, relieving us of the hassle of moving our arthritis-ridden, aging bodies around so much.

These sorts of creative solutions to how we want to live as we get older are often more available than we think.

Unfortunately, many of us are too caught up in the cult of independence to see these possibilities; either we don't wish to be a burden on others, or we don't wish to be burdened *by* others. Either way, we find ourselves more isolated than we need to be. In speaking with hundreds of elderly people, I've noticed a distinct pattern of loneliness among those vaunting their own independence. We become Eleanor Rigbys, waiting at the windows of life. The "achievement" of living on one's own is diminished by the sense of being ignored or left behind. This diminishment can become a barrier standing between our Egos and the rest of the world, increasingly solid and hard to cross. Whether through shame over our own aging, or through fear of dependency, we should be vigilant about this tendency to isolate ourselves as we get older. To offset it, we might seek out community centers and other meeting places where peers congregate, or consider alternative living arrangements such as assisted-living centers, spiritual communities, and multiple-age communities set up specifically for bringing people of all generations together.

THE WISDOM OF DEPENDENCY

Dependency is a big hurdle for most people, especially given the values of our society. Being dependent, needing help, makes us feel diminished, because we value self-sufficiency and independence so highly. We value taking care of others, but shun the notion of being taken care of ourselves. I certainly have confronted this issue a great deal since my stroke, and have learned firsthand how difficult the Ego can make it for us. At first, it was hard for me. I had to confront those aspects that made me want to hold myself separate and not accept help. This willful, stubborn part of the Ego develops in the period known as the Terrible Twos, when the child first refuses to be aided by its parents, and it persists without our knowing it as we age. If we've never developed a way of asking for help, this is going to be a difficult hurdle to clear; if needing someone else embarrasses us, or gives rise to feelings of humiliation, we may well deny the need for help as long as we can. Rather than opening our hands to accept what others have to offer, many of us close down when we have to ask for something, making it hard to be grateful, and creating a situation that's no fun for anybody. What I've found, in fact, is that when there is true surrender and service between people, the roles of helper and helped, and the boundaries between those in power and those who are powerless, begin to dissolve.

Situations in which we become dependent can become transformative experiences for all parties concerned. By allowing ourselves to reveal our need, we allow those around us the opportunity to help, which is a fundamental need we all share. By being open about our own dependency, we can help those around us to become free of *their* own fear of dependency. On the other hand, if we demonstrate resistance or anger over dependency, we create suffering, causing our caretakers to become uncomfortable in reaction to our feelings. Instead of an honest exchange, such situations can become farcical, with both parties pretending not to be playing the roles they're playing.

If you have to be dependent, you can learn to be joyfully dependent. This wasn't so easy for me, but I'm making the shift. Becoming unable to drive helped me do this. I have always loved my cars. A friend of mine had a beautiful BMW, "the ultimate driving machine," and I loved the drives we took in it. It was such a fantastic car that I finally bought it from her. I had the stroke before I had a chance to drive it. I fantasized about driving that car, and had it fixed up—but then I got "fixed up." My caretakers would tell me what a wonderful car it was to drive, and I would get excited about it until I realized that I would have to be chauffeured if I ever wanted to ride in it. That made me a little cranky, and jealous of others' ability to drive. That in turn made them uncomfortable. They'd feel a little guilty because they could do something I couldn't. One day, something in my attitude shifted. Instead of thinking, "Oh, poor me, I can't drive," I thought, "Oh boy! I'm going to have a chauffeur in my Beemer! Now I'm free to look around at the scenery." Because I enjoyed the trip, the people who helped me were able to enjoy it as well. My happiness led to their happiness.

If we view the dependent situation from a Soul perspective, we realize how liberating it can be. Rather than being trapped in our Ego's version of power and powerlessness, what we see from this perspective is Souls engaged in a sacred exchange of love and care. Rather than resenting our dependency or blaming ourselves for not being as independent as we once were, we see our new circumstance as an opportunity for greater intimacy.

Before my stroke, I would never have dreamed I could be as peaceful as I am with the attention of other people, or that I could allow people to "invade my privacy" to the degree that I have, but these experiences have touched me very deeply. This is the paradox of what we call misfortune: that so often what we most resist bestows on our lives the greatest, most unexpected blessings. I do not mean this in a Pollyanna sense—none of us, including myself, would wish to be overly dependent on others, or to be unable to care for ourselves. I mean simply to acknowledge that when such role changes come to pass, we're often surprised by benefits, and deep learning, that we would not have anticipated.

When you meet someone who is dependent but who's not caught in all those traps, it's amazing how light and delightful their dependency becomes. People who take care of someone who's dependent in that way come away feeling they've received a gift. And isn't that really the game of human relationships—that when we walk away, we both feel gifted from having been in the exchange? After all, when we look at incarnation from the Soul view, we see that our human interactions aren't just about surviving; nor are they only about getting food or shelter, about care-giving or care-receiving. They're about mirroring each other's hearts. All the other stuff is window dressing; it's the medium through which the important interaction takes place. Rob Lehman, a fine friend, wrote in a letter to me, "Providing ways to help and support each other on our journeys to truth may be the highest form of love."

Opening ourselves to the needs of others, and allowing ourselves to be honest about our own changing needs as we get older, requires what Suzuki Roshi, a Buddhist monk, terms "beginner's mind": the ability to respond freshly to each moment as it arises, without undue prejudice or expectation. Often, our resistance to asking for help stems from not wanting to be a bother to anyone. But what do we mean by being a "bother", or by being "bothered" by the needs of others? In order to become mindful of our needs and the needs of those around us, we must begin to examine our attachment to the way we believe things ought to be, and the picture we carry of who we are and what we ought to be doing. I crossed this bridge myself when my father became too ill to take care of himself and my step-mother asked me to come help out. At first, I couldn't help but view Dad's illness as an intrusion on my life, and on all the things I wanted to be doing. I had plans and expectations in which my father's dependency was not a part. And yet, I could not refuse my duty; my father had given me life and now he needed somebody to take care of him. Though I was in my 50s, I was unmarried and could change my life more easily than the rest of the family could. But this was not a simple surrender. From the Sixties onward, I'd spent a great deal of energy push-ing my family away. Each time I'd return from India after doing intensive spiritual practice, my Dad would ask me if I had a job yet. I resigned myself to the fact that he would never understand me. But here he was in his 80s, frail and in need of my help. So I went back and lived in a little apartment in the basement of the house where my father and stepmother were living. At first I did this grudgingly, thinking of the "sacrifice" I was making, buying into people's praise over what a good son I was to be caring for Dad so nicely. But as time went on, my egotistical attachment to my role as caretaker began to fade, until finally Dad and I were just two people hanging out together, father and son to be sure, but more than that, Souls exchanging love. The fact that there was dependency was no longer the issue. By the time Dad died, I realized that I'd been given an incredible gift, and was extremely grateful for having been shaken out of my egocentric attachment to external "freedom" and the way I thought my life was supposed to be. What had happened between us seemed deeply appropriate. Caring for Dad, as he had cared for me when I was a child, gave me a sense of harmony and completion.

HOLDING ON TO POWER

The Ego derives its identity from the roles it plays as an actor in the world. One of its primary motivations for playing these roles is power. For this reason, it is essential that we become mindful of where our attachment to power lies, in order to relieve the sense of loss and suffering as we age.

We measure power by many criteria: how much money we have in the bank, how many shares of stock we own, how physically attractive we are, how much authority we wield over how many people, how much we are in control of our own destiny. But regardless of the object of attachment, these power "signs" all contain the ability to entrap us. As we get older and the external proofs of power begin to slip away, we become aware of the degree of our entrapment, and of the futility of trying to cling to these worldly assurances.

I've often been struck by the poignancy of meeting old people of great wealth and power, and seeing how frightened they are of losing what they have. The greater their clinging, the greater their pain, realizing how little use the accoutrements of power and worldly position are in helping them age with wisdom and peace. In truth, the Ego's attachment to power of any kind is linked inextricably to the fear of losing that power, and thus becomes a source of suffering.

There is a kind of power that does not give rise to fear, however. It is spiritual power, the power of the enlightened mind. As we begin to emphasize Soul power over worldly power, our perception of the alterations brought on by aging changes proportionately. I can remember sitting with my guru one day when Indira Gandhi, the Prime Minister of India, went by at some little distance with her whole retinue of limousines and trucks and jeeps and generals. There sat Maharajji—this old man on a wooden bench with his blanket wrapped around him—shaking his head and smiling. "Look at all that," he said, "and it's just for a *worldly* king." At that moment, viewed from a spiritual point of view, the pomp and circumstance seemed silly, rather like a game of little tin soldiers. Because it was transitory, this worldly power is not real, he seemed to be saying, and therefore it gives rise to fear that it will be lost.

Years back, I had a humbling experience that taught me this lesson firsthand. I was vacationing on Martha's Vineyard with Tara and Danny Goleman, who's like my younger guru-brother. Danny's book, *Emotional Intelligence*, had been on the *New York Times* bestsellers list for many months. We were walking down the beach, where I was used to being recognized and made much of. A man came up to us and said, "You look familiar." I started to smile and look appropriately humble. Then he said, "Aren't you Dan Goleman?" I realized he wasn't talking to me at all! My humble smile froze on my face. Then the man asked Danny, referring to me, "Is this your father?" Needless to say, my attachment to the role of social star was shaken to the ground in an instant!

RETIREMENT ANXIETY

Retirement is a common focus for our fear of losing power and position in the world. Besides giving us a feeling of power, our jobs help to structure our days and to make us feel needed. Since many of us have been trained to see ourselves as what we do for a living, we're haunted by a feeling of uselessness when those work roles are taken away. I recall in my teens playing gin rummy with one of my father's friends, a seventy-six-year-old chairman of a large textile empire, who was complaining bitterly about the headaches of moving all his mills out of New England in search of cheaper labor in the South. I asked him why, wealthy as he was, he felt he had to do all this. Why not retire and enjoy himself—let someone else do it? His poignant reply was that he didn't know what else to do. Similarly, the great tycoon Andrew Carnegie, when asked why he kept working, replied, "I've forgotten how to do anything else." Though the context was different, their predicament was like that of the ancient Chinese man who had carried firewood all his life and was asked if there was anything he was sorry about; he answered that he was only sorry that he had nothing left to carry. Three years ago, I was visiting with a ninety-two-year-old who prides himself on working the same schedule he has followed for the past forty-five years. He sees himself as a role model, seeing clients each day, but I couldn't help but see a more poignant dimension to his success. For although he had managed to hold on to his role—and was genuinely interested in helping people—it struck me that without his work (which aging could take from him at any time), he would be lost. His inability to allow for change in his self-image was moving, of course—and courageous from an Ego point of view—but disquieting from a Soul perspective.

In each of these instances we hear the fear of disempowered role-lessness; the fear of having nothing structured, nothing we're "supposed" to be doing, that becomes so palpable around retirement time. To counteract their anxiety, people often throw themselves into other activities, such as volunteerism, second families, vacationing that never ends, or hobbies and avocations, to maintain a sense of having some purpose. Though there's certainly nothing wrong with being busy, the desperation that often prompts these activities does create a shadow. In other words, it is often more skillful to be still and attend to the frightening feelings that a change such as retirement can arouse in us than to rush to fill the free time in order to avoid our feelings. We have the opportunity to ask ourselves why we fear inactivity, and what feelings we avoid by our perpetual busy-ness. Rather than being overwhelmed by our fears, we may discover that they are founded on misconceptions, or assumptions, and that the fears are far worse than the reality they cling to. We may discover that we have prejudices of which we're unaware about how it's worthwhile to spend our time. As Gay Luce has noted, "After having been applauded for busy-ness and productivity, there is guilt about stillness." This attitude is endemic to our materialistic, youth-oriented culture, and counterproductive to our approach to conscious aging, which requires a great deal of stillness in order to awaken to the wisdom within us.

Rather than view retirement as the end of the line, it is possible to see it as an opportunity. Though the shift may be confusing and frightening at first, I have seen it give way to delight and a sense of freedom time and again. Often, people who've held to their roles as working citizens with the greatest tenacity release their hold with the greatest relief, and learn to channel their energies in new and surprising directions. For some, like eighty-three-year-old Florida Scott-Maxwell, this means settling more comfortably into an elder station of life. As she writes, "Age forces us to deal with idleness, emptiness, not being needed, not able to do . . . Now that I am sure that this freedom is the right garnering of age, I am so busy being old that I dread interruptions." For other retirees, idleness is a less-appealing path. During the fall of 1995, I spent four days at the

Gorbachev World Forum, where I met some remarkable elder role models who were taking part in that program, among them Barbara Weidner, a Catholic woman in her 80s who heads an organization called "Grandmothers for Peace." When I asked her why she'd gotten involved with the peace movement, she said, "I just started to think: 'What kind of world am I leaving for my grandchildren?' And I wasn't very happy with what I saw. So I decided I'd better speak up and do something about it."

"So," she said, "I made a sign. It read 'A Grandmother for Peace.' And I went and stood places with it, just making my statement. And then one day, I found myself kneeling with others as part of a human barrier on the road in front of a munitions truck during a protest at a weapons facility. I was arrested, I was taken to prison, I was strip-searched, and I was left in a cell. And at that moment," she said, "something happened to me. I realized they couldn't do anything more to me. I was free."

Since then, Barbara has been all over the world, aligning herself with grandmothers everywhere, bringing her message of peace. She's been with the Zapatistas in the mountains of Chiapas, Mexico. She's been in the war zones in Nicaragua and Chechnya. She was at the Women's Conference in Beijing. To the grandmothers she says, "Our power is just the force of our love for our children and grandchildren." What I saw represented in her were precisely the qualities of elder wisdom that our world needs, the unique gift that only an older person, in this case a grandmother, can contribute, a compassion that comes not out of righteousness, but out of the maturity of her connectedness with the rhythms of the universe. Barbara's work demonstrates as well the power of the heart, as opposed to the Ego, that worldly retirement does nothing to diminish.

Working with the ill and dying is another task for which wise elders are uniquely suited. Having done this work intensively for the past thirty years, I've learned an enormous amount about myself and those whose bedsides I've attended; in fact, I have often felt like the student being taught by the people whose suffering I have witnessed. What more perfect role could we have, as people facing our own aging and death, than that of being with others in the same position? Three years ago, while speaking at a conference in Brazil, I made an offhand remark that I later thought was important. There is a relationship between what we need to learn, and what we do in the world. I said, "It's interesting when you stop thinking of spiritual practice as what you do on your meditation cushion, and realize that your karma is your dharma." In other words, what we do in the world—our *dharma*—*is* our spiritual practice. The reaction to this remark was startling. Dozens of people approached me afterward to say that this idea had rung true for them, and helped them to see the roles they were playing in the world quite differently.

In the face of our culture's dismissal of roles and activities that do not contribute to "productivity," it's important that we be mindful of separating our values, as wise elders, from the values of those around us. Although there are exceptions like Barbara Weidner, most of us cannot expect kudos for participating in the sorts of activities that appeal to us in older age; there are no awards for planting gardens, or playing with our grandchildren, or taking stock of our lives; no social "payback" for practicing mindfulness, becoming conscious of our fears, unloosing the mental knots of lifetimes spent striving and achieving. As we age, it is helpful to begin to release our need for social approval; indeed, as many older people have told me, one of the primary gifts of old age is no longer caring so much what others think of us, and feeling free to be ourselves. Ideally, this process of freeing ourselves from cultural expectations, and becoming mindful of our true values, can begin long before we enter old age, so that our inner resources are strengthened when we need them later on.

Fortunately, this has been the case in my own life. When I was on the faculty at Harvard, I taught a course in career counseling, and invited students to tailor their career planning to the roles that best reflected their own values and capabilities. However, after I was fired from the university, and, in effect, from academia, I found myself faced with the challenge of applying what I was preaching. I looked carefully at my values and determined what roles I could grow into in my personal and professional life, and made a series of decisions that affected the course of the next thirty years. I decided that in the family realm, I would assume the uncle role; in politics and commerce, I would play the advisor-fool to the court; and in the larger society, I would assume the part of the social philosopher. I wanted to be free of the power pecking order, I realized, and move toward a vision of myself as Ram Dass, wise man.

Part of the appeal of this approach was that my career possibilities would not be limited by my age. The older I got, the more I felt myself growing into the "role-less role" I'd chosen. As the years went on, I refined my job to correspond with what the people who came to hear me thought that they needed, which was, essentially, a mouth to verbalize the wisdom we all share. In fact, I frequently began my lectures by saying, "Good evening ladies and gentlemen. My name is Ram Dass. In India that means servant of God, and is another name for Hanuman, the monkey-God who lives only to serve Ram. But in recent years, I have come to take the letters RAM as an acronym for Rent-A-Mouth. I figure that this evening you rented my mouth to say back to you what you already know. How do I know you know? Because when I say something that I think is particularly wise or far out, you nod knowingly. If you didn't know, why would you nod? And if you do know, why do you need to hire me? The only conclusion I've been able to draw so far is that out of some evolutionary necessity we need to keep saying it to ourselves over and over again until we hear it." It works.

But while such a function gave me a place in society, however marginal, I tried to hold it lightly, knowing that it could be taken away at any time. Since having my stroke, for instance, I feel less able, and less inclined, to speak publicly, and though there have been times when I miss being more in the public eye, I'm grateful not to have become overly attached to my job. To cling too tightly to a fixed image of what a wise elder says and does is fundamentally unwise, after all. As we learn to age more consciously, we become increasingly mindful of the impermanent nature of all worldly things, including the voice that we offer to the world. Understanding our positions in the greater scheme of life, and learning to separate personal power from spiritual power, is a crucial step in Soul maturity.

ECCENTRICITY

At one point in his life, Gandhi was leading a protest march against the tyranny of the British Empire. Thousands of Indian people were involved; they'd left their jobs and come long distances to take part in the demonstration, but at a certain point when violence was about to break out Gandhi ordered his lieutenants to cancel the march and to disperse the crowd. The people protested and begged Gandhi to reconsider, but his reply revealed the humility of a lifetime spent in spiritual practice. "God is absolute truth," he said. "I am a human; I only understand relative truth. So, my understanding of truth can change from day to day. And my commitment must be to truth rather than to consistency."

In this same way, confronted by old age's slings and arrows, we must allow ourselves to be "inconsistent" from a conventional point of view, and adjust our plans and attitudes as our needs change. Since old age is sure to bring us many surprises, we should learn to be more flexible in our behavior, rather than more rigid. As Emerson wrote, "A foolish consistency is the hobgoblin of little minds," and in fact the freedom to be inconsistent is one of old age's greatest blessings. We're free to be "eccentric" and improvise as we go along. We're free to be a little "dotty," and free ourselves from conventional behavior. There are two quotes that I always keep close by that reflect the sort of thing I mean. The first was written by Nadine Stair, an eighty-five-year-old woman:

> "If I had my life to live over, I'd like to make more mistakes next time. I'd relax. I'd limber up. I'd be sillier than I've been this trip. I would take fewer things seriously. I'd take more chances. I'd climb more mountains and swim more rivers. I'd eat more ice cream and less beans. I would perhaps have more troubles, but I'd have fewer imaginary ones. You see, I'm one of those people who lived sensibly and sanely, hour after hour, day after day. Oh, I've had my moments . . . and if I had it to do over again I'd have more of them. In fact I'd try to have nothing else—just moments, one after another, instead of living so many years ahead of each day. I've been one of those persons who never goes anywhere without a thermometer, a hot water bottle, a raincoat, and a parachute. If I had it to do again I'd travel lighter

than I have. If I had my life to live over, I'd start bare-foot earlier in the spring, stay that way later in the fall. I'd go to more dances. I'd ride more merry-go-rounds. I'd pick more daisies. I would live each moment more."

The second is a poem by Jenny Joseph about the way she intends to delight in the playful eccentricity of her age. It's called *Warning*:

> When I am an old woman, I shall wear purple
> With a red hat, which doesn't go,
> And doesn't suit me.
> And I shall spend my pension on brandy
> And summer gloves and satin sandals
> And say, "We've no money for butter."

> I shall sit down on the pavement when I'm tired.
> And gobble up samples in shops,
> And press alarm bells,
> And run my stick along the public railings,
> And make up for the sobriety of my youth.
> I shall go out in my slippers in the rain,
> And pick the flowers in other people's gardens,
> And learn to spit.

> You can wear terrible shirts,
> And grow more fat,
> And eat three pounds of sausages at a go,
> Or only bread and pickles for a week,
> And hoard pens and pencils and beer-mats
> And things in boxes.

Yes, but now we must have clothes to keep us dry,
And pay the rent
And not swear in the street,
And set a good example for the children,
And must have friends to dinner,
And read the papers.
But maybe I ought to practice a little now,
So people who know me are not too shocked
and surprised
When suddenly I am old and start to wear purple.

THE LIFE WITHIN

In the elderly, two sets of values operate simultaneously: the desire to stay active and to maintain a sense of self-worth in the eyes of others, and the desire to withdraw from social commitments to a more leisurely, contemplative life. Although this inward-turning is viewed by some as antisocial, a problem to be solved or worried about ("I used to be so active, what's wrong with me?"), it seems to be a natural by-product of aging. This isn't a paranoid drawing-inward, it isn't being afraid of the world, but rather a kind of deepening that seems to result from the nearness of death, and the desire to reflect on what life is all about.

It is important to create opportunities for doing that—to build some time into our lives to consider our deepest questions about who we are, where we are, and how it all makes sense. It's a great feeling to be able to open the door to mystery and reflect on the deeper significance of life. Slowing down is the only way to take advantage of this opportunity.

I receive a lot of letters from spiritual seekers who tell me that they're lonely on their path, live in small towns and have no one around with whom to share how they're feeling. They're looking for fellowship, a community of like-minded Souls with whom to voice their concerns about the deeper issues surrounding aging, the mystery of death, and how to remain conscious in the face of physical, social and psychological challenges. Community is vital to help us reorient ourselves to a spiritual perspective. It helps to have fellow seekers in your life who can help you to stay on-track, and who remind you gently when you seem to have lost your way. Being in the company of people engaged in conscious-aging practice helps strengthen our resolve, and helps us stand firm against the cultural messages that conspire against elder wisdom.

It's important for us to seek out opportunities for connecting with others on this path of wisdom, and when this isn't possible, to find other ways to cultivate some means of staying connected. Books are an excellent tool for maintaining such support; in the years when I traveled a great deal and couldn't always be in the company of others on a conscious path, I kept a cache of reliable book-friends with me: the quotes of Lao Tzu, the *Dhammapada* or the *Gita*, as a lifeline to wisdom. I have a very dear friend whose grandmother is a Christian Scientist; although a very worldly person, she reads the literature of her faith every day without fail, and has done so for many years. Although her family is worried that this faith might compromise her willingness to accept medical treatment as she gets older, this lady seems quite happy, and uses her spiritual studies to remain grounded in a Soul perspective

Our relationship with the world at large shifts from "outer" to "inner." We learn, as our worldly roles fall away, to place emphasis on connections of the heart. We come to recognize and honor our relationships with family, friends, and the greater community. Although we may remain active in our communities, we do not forget that old age is a time for reflection and inner work. Free of the pressure to achieve, and of the masks we've worn to operate in society, we focus our attention on remaining mindful of each precious passing day, and on not becoming entangled in the voices of our Ego. Equipped with this wisdom we find ourselves free to live more creatively than ever before. We create our lives from a place of equanimity and peace, from the quiet spaciousness of being awake, and in love, among all living things.

6

LIVING
IN THE
PRESENT
MOMENT

I n this chapter, we will focus on how to work with time. We will examine how our preoccupations with the past and the future take us out of this present moment, depriving us of joy and Awareness, and how our conscious aging can be used to awaken us; to steady us in the flux of time. Finally, we will turn our attention to the oftentimes-difficult topic of change—which only accelerates as we get older—and to how to respond to change in a wise and balanced manner.

THE LAW OF IMPERMANENCE

Back in 1970, I first began to practice Buddhist meditation systematically at a course in Bodh Gaya, India. It was there, five hundred years before the birth of Christ, that the Buddha sat under the Bodhi tree and became enlightened.

One of the first things that I was taught, the very cornerstone of Buddhist practice, in fact, was regarding the impermanence of all phenomena; the doctrine known as *anicca*. This was not an entirely new concept to me; in my practice of taking entheogens such as LSD, I had often experienced the dissolution of what seemed, to the ordinary eye, solid and permanent. Also, growing up in the West, I was familiar with the biblical injunction not to "lay up our treasure where moth and rust doth corrupt." But it was in this meditative setting that I first began to deeply consider the transitory nature of phenomena.

Historically, monks in that Buddhist tradition carried out

their training in the charnel grounds, where the bodies of the dead were thrown to be eaten by birds and other animals. There, the monks would sit all night and meditate upon the different stages of the decaying bodies—from the bloated corpse, to the skeleton, to the dust of the bones that was left when everything else was gone. This practice helped the monks to fully grasp the impermanent nature of not only the physical body, but of all material life, and thus to disengage their attachment to the physical realm—to learn to witness the mind and body from a Soul level. By learning to be fully present in the moment, and to observe the rushing stream of change from a still and centered point, these meditators gained the insight that we can aspire to as we age. In developing non-attachment toward the body, and in turn toward all change in the material environment, the monks were given a glimpse of liberation, a doorway through which their Awareness could travel in order to be free of the suffering we associate with the passage of time.

Although this particular "cemetery meditation" is not available to us in the West (though it still goes on in other places around the world), the intensive practice at Bodh Gaya did sensitize me to the fact of impermanence, and to the way we usually attempt to avoid it. This recognition of impermanence brought great anxiety; it revealed the fragility of the place upon which I was trying to stand. My Ego balked at the truth; built on the illusion of its own solid, separate existence, it fought the overwhelming evidence that it, like everything else, was impermanent (we might even say fictitious). It brought to my mind Shelley's poem "Ozymandias," in which the speaker discovers the ruin of a colossal statue in the desert. Nearby lies a stone marked with this inscription: "'I am Ozymandias, king of kings: Look on my works, ye Mighty, and despair!'" But, the next lines reveal, "Nothing beside remains. . . . The lone and level sands stretch far away." The

Ego, imagining itself immortal, the ruler in its self-made kingdom, is shaken to its foundations by the inescapable nature of change.

This stroke has given me a unique perspective on time. Although once I could guess the time to the very minute, now I find it difficult sometimes to remember what day of the week it is, or even what season of the year. Because my memory has been affected, I'm forced to live in the present moment so intensely that I sometimes forget where I've been from day to day. This is disorienting when it happens—at times, it's downright exasperating—but on the positive side, it keeps me walking the talk of the practice that I'm recommending. I'm no longer bound to past and future in the same way, and the relief from this is tremendous. For this reason, illness (and aging in general) contains the seeds of great opportunity in terms of spiritual growth. By making stillness *necessary*, it slows us down to here-and-now. Although I would like my memory back, I recognize the advantages of my brain's current limitation and use it to fully enter the present.

We can use devices like watching our breathing to begin to enter the present moment and break the time-binding traps we've set for ourselves. You can free yourself from worrying about the past and from anxiety about what's to come in the future by fully entering the present moment. When you deepen into a moment, you disappear—at least, the solid "you" that you're used to experiencing disappears. Everything around you—maybe it's a palm tree, dripping water, cars honking, people racing past you—everything feels ecstatic when you free yourself into the moment. You recognize your interconnectedness, and all these things in a moment can become mystical doorways for the Soul. In this state, you can't worry about the past or the future, and you can't worry about "me," because you can no longer find a separate "me." In the moment, we become free from the Ego's desires and open to the Soul. We break the time-binding and interrupt the Ego melodrama. The soap opera takes a commercial break for a message from our sponsor: God.

RELEASING THE PAST, FORGETTING THE FUTURE

The following stanza from the Tibetan school of Buddhism will help us begin our practice of looking at time and change through new eyes:

Prolong not the past.
Invite not the future.
Alter not your innate wakefulness.
Don't fear appearances.
There is nothing more than that.

As we get older, the tendency to dwell in the past becomes more enticing. With less to occupy our days, and less of a future to anticipate, we fill our minds with recollections and nostalgia, poring back over the years, sometimes tenderly, at other times with regret, anger, longing, or sadness, coloring our present lives with baggage and memories. Although this is understandable, it is important that we become aware of when reminiscence becomes an obstacle, or a burden, and of the degree to which we identify with who we've been in previous time. It is impossible to be present if you're trapped in personal history. And what, after all, is the difference between the past and a dream?

Letting go of personal history doesn't mean denying it; it means not allowing it to color the present moment with past experience. For example, I used to say, "I'm a golfer, and a sports-car driver." That's my personal history. But now I'm someone telling that story. I can't golf or drive anymore. If I cling to that identity, I suffer. I can still tell stories, but I have to tell them without becoming the person I was when I golfed and drove cars. The things I did were exciting to that person, but they don't grip me in the same way. I have let go. You can bring your past up to your consciousness and look at it with the eyes of the present. Any memory can be captivating, but you have to bring it back to who you are in the present to nullify its grip on you.

Unless we make a conscious effort to live with "beginner's mind," coming to each experience fresh, we find that the accumulation of our years can become a ball and chain. Let me give you an example. In 1979, I was living in Soquel, California. I had been wandering for the past few years, following my guru's injunction not to stay in one place for too long, since "yogis and water go bad if they don't keep moving," but in spite of my gypsy life I had continued to collect memorabilia. The stuff I'd gathered was interesting (at least to me): old letters, pictures, newspaper clippings, license plates—boxes and boxes of mementos I couldn't bear to throw away.

This tendency to drag my belongings from the past with me was not really suited to a yogi's life. In the Hindu tradition of the wandering *sadhu*, of which Maharajji was an example, one isn't burdened by material possessions at all. At one stage in his life, my guru was called "Cracked Pot Baba," because he went around naked with no possessions other than an old cracked pot that someone had discarded, which he used to beg with and to hold food and water. When one pot would break, he'd throw it away and pick up another. Of course, living in the States, I had no intention of imitating Maharajji, but here I was, a wandering sadhu, lugging my memorabilia around. Of course, I almost never opened any of these boxes; I simply filled them, labeled them, sealed them up and put them on a shelf. Then, when it came time to move, I'd haul down this mountain of big boxes, load up the Rider truck and move it all to the next apartment. After doing this four or five times, I began to ask myself

"What is this about? Why am I saving all this stuff?" As I thought about it, I realized that I was saving it under the illusion that later on I would miss it. Although I didn't need any of these things at the moment, I was sure I would, somewhere down the line. Truthfully, although life was exciting at the moment, I was anticipating that later on it would get boring. Though I had enough to keep me occupied now, the photographs from that wonderful trip to the canyon in 1965 would surely be useful someday. I imagined myself relying on these old boxes to remind me of what my life had been. Then one day this struck me as absurd! I pulled the boxes off the shelves and carried them out to the trash cans. At first, I felt righteous and wise: I'd freed myself of ballast, now I could sail on without that weight. But then in the middle of the night, I found myself out rummaging through the garbage pails, having remembered this or that thing that I simply couldn't live without. "I'll never see that person's face again!" I thought, frantically searching in the dark. Then it hit me that I was defeating the purpose of what I'd done, and that I couldn't trust myself to leave all these things in the garbage can. *I would have to burn them.*

I built a big fire in the fireplace and sat in front of it with all my boxes. One by one, I opened them and said goodbye to each thing inside the box, then put it in the fire and let it go. Now and then I'd come across something too precious to burn, like pictures of my guru, and I put these relics aside. But for the most part, I incinerated all of my memorabilia. It was a radical, scary feeling. I was frightened that I'd grieve later on for what I'd done. But although over the years I've occasionally damned myself for what I did, when I've been asked to produce a picture of this or that and realized that the only one went up in smoke, I've mostly felt freer at having relieved myself of this weight of the past. But having relieved myself of this weight of the past, I also felt freer.

Fifteen years later, my basement is full of boxes again. It's time for another fire.

I'm not implying that we should discard or forget our past. There's nothing wrong with taking pleasure in the story of who we've been, provided this identification with the past does not obscure the present, or cause us suffering through clinging to something that isn't anymore and lamenting over its loss.

We must be aware, though, of the tendency to milk our own biographies for entertainment or sympathy value. For example, I used to fly an airplane and have had adventures that can put listeners on the edge of their seats. It's a wonder I'm alive, truly, and over a beer I can tell many a hair-raising story. But when I do this, I notice an interesting thing: I feel as if I'm turning into somebody else. I'm no longer Ram Dass today, but rather that other, daredevil character, and attractive as that sometimes seems to my Ego, it also traps me in a past identity, and feels a trifle inauthentic.

As we learn to be more conscious of the aging process, it helps to pay attention to this feeling of being "an impostor," caught halfway between earlier days and who we are in this moment. The more we come to peace with ourselves as elderly people, bearers of memories *but not the memories themselves*, the more alive we will feel.

UNFINISHED BUSINESS

The work of releasing the past is not easy, however, especially when our minds are preoccupied with "unfinished business." It is a paradox of mindful living that without having embraced our past, we cannot let it go; or, as a sage once said, "we cannot transform what we have not first blessed." As I discovered in my attempt to release my belongings, I could not let go of these things without having looked at each one, acknowledged the memory fully, before putting it into the fire.

There's a great difference between wallowing in the past, turning each detail over endlessly in one's mind until one is stuck there, and "experiencing" it with one's present consciousness. In India, I developed a practice of sitting by a stream and watching the leaves go by, then observing the thoughts (memories) of my mind in the same way: there was my mother's death, there was my first love affair, there was being thrown out of Harvard, there was meeting my guru; memory after memory, floating by like leaves. I began to see certain things through eyes of the present. For example, being thrown out of Harvard took away the secure professor role from my Ego. Now I saw the karmic weave of these events, the way the culture pushed me out of my institutional nest. It was falling out of that tree that helped me learn to trust my inner voice. An Ego thing was turned into a Soul thing. My creativity was released when the identity of Harvard professor was ripped away. Creativity comes from the Soul. When we're bound by institutions, we can't think rebelliously. I wasn't allowed to think about opening my mind with LSD.

By embracing the past into the present, our minds are able to enter a kind of choiceless Awareness in which past experience can float up and pass away, with no clinging or judgment. When we do that, the memories get "neutralized"; they become part of the backdrop of existence, and the energy that has been locked into holding onto the past is released. We feel a little freer, a little more alive.

If we don't maintain that "wisdom distance," it's nearly impossible to confront painful or traumatic events, or the deep regret of "roads not taken," without becoming stuck in rage or self-pity. In other words, we bring present consciousness to bear on past events, and thus bring the past *into the present moment*. Turning our attention this way, with the strength of our conscious minds, we make the past release its hold on us, and we feel a shift away from old attachments.

What we discover, once we learn to look at the past through the eyes of the present, is the degree to which our thoughts and feelings have been frozen in time. Although *we* may have changed tremendously with age, we carry with us the interpretation, and emotional effect, of past events as they occurred *then*. Is it any wonder that we feel fragmented? We need to learn to "re-experience" memories and feelings from the Soul's perspective.

There are moments we can remember in our lives when we did step into the Soul's perspective. The times we've been fully conscious stick out as different from other memories we carry. They act as mirrors to show us who we really are. My guru once said about my mother, "She is a very high Soul." I asked the translator, "Did Maharajji say 'is' or 'was'?" The translator replied, "He said 'is.'" My mother was already dead when this happened. This understanding gave me a different orientation to my relationship with my mother, one I had glimpsed only rarely as a child. When I was eight or nine, she and I were in the car together. We were playing a game of seeing who could sing a note and hold it the longest. A man pulled up next to us and stared at this spectacle. In that moment of shared embarrassment we were catapulted from our roles as mother and son into the roles of two troublemakers. Linked by the experience of that moment, which had nothing to do with being parent and child, we were able to perceive each other as Souls.

And again, when I was about thirty-five and my mother was dying, we had a moment when we looked at each other as just two Souls. When everyone else was lying to her about her condition, I was able to say to her, "You're dying. You remind me of a friend who's in a burning building. This building will be consumed. You'll go on, and I'll go on." We had a deep Soul-to-Soul talk that day.

Some years ago, I had a very strange experience in Hawaii. I had received a letter saying there were some people there who wanted me to come and meditate with them, and since I was already planning to speak on Maui and Kauai, I decided to stop off on the Big Island on the way. I was met by a rather strange group of people—they didn't talk to me at all. They led me to the car and drove me to a coffee plantation way up in the mountains.

When I got there, I rested for a while and then was taken to the office of the man who ran the center. I walked in and the man looked at me and said, "Uhvuh, vuhva, va?" Well, I didn't understand. I just looked at him blankly. He said it again and it was clear that I was supposed to do *something*. I decided to play it safe and say, "*Om*." He said, "Uh, vah, vah!" I thought, "Hm-mmm . . . I guess we are going to create a new language to-gether." So we did that for a while, and then a young woman brought us a plate of fruit, and the man said, "Well, I think we are ready to begin now." I thought to myself, "Begin what?" He then drew aside a big curtain that constituted one of the walls and there were thirty people sitting there silently. They all looked at me and waited for me to speak.

I had nothing planned; I had not planned to lecture. But I started to say something or other, trying to be charming, my usual thing. After a few minutes, someone raised his hand and said, "Ram Dass, I really treasured *Be Here Now*. Why aren't you like your book?" I fumbled with that one a bit, and spoke for a few minutes more, and then a woman said, "Ram Dass, I don't feel any heart from you." Well, then I was defensive. I said, "What do you mean you don't feel any heart? That's your problem, not mine." And we were off. We sat for hours talking, with me using my wit and cleverness to convince them that I was okay. At around 11:30 P.M., the doctor who led the group said, "Well, I think we have gone as far as we can go tonight. We'll begin at 7:30 tomorrow morning." I thought, "What am I going to do? I'm trapped on a mountain with these lunatics!"

I went back to my room and thought about it. I looked out at the stars and the bougainvillea and reflected about the evening. I realized that they were pushing my buttons—but they were right. I was in my head, and I could well understand how that might be blocking them from feeling my heart. I was being charming but I was not really being straight with them.

The next morning I walked in and I said, "You are absolutely right. Please help me." They started to get me to talk about this and that (it turned out they were a therapeutic community, not a meditation center), and soon they had me lying down on the floor, doing a session in primal regression. Within a very short time, I was making fists and screaming with rage while they all sat around me pressing their hands down on my body. I felt as if I were back in my crib: I could see the window, the bars of the crib, the pattern of sunlight, the whole scene surrounding me as an infant. As my temper tantrum continued, mother was next to me with her hand on my chest, holding me down, looking at me with great coldness. I remembered the feeling that my power was being overwhelmed, and that I was somehow being defeated by her. By re-experiencing that domination through my present state of consciousness, I was able to see that I'd built a whole personality structure *in reaction to* this primal experience, a personality in which I had to placate the world around me in order for people to love me and give me power. They had to *give* me power—it wasn't *my* power; it was theirs to give or withhold.

Remembering that episode freed up something deep inside of me, but I wouldn't have been able to relive it and bring it up to date in my consciousness without the help of that strange group. We all carry the imprint of past experiences in our emotional memories, many of which occurred in our pre-verbal times. As we age, we often feel closer to these early experiences than we have for many years. With more time for reflection, our minds venture back toward the beginning and the traumas that may have occurred there. This gives us an excellent opportunity to clean house, and bring wisdom to bear on these early wounds.

Part of our conscious-aging curriculum, then, is to allow ourselves to reflect upon our past through the eyes of the present, in order to awaken ourselves to who we are now. If you discover that certain experiences in particular return to your thoughts, practice reflecting upon them during your meditation; rather than following the breath as the primary object of mindfulness, allow yourself to follow the thoughts and sensations surrounding the memory, being careful to remain conscious of where you are in the present moment. You can use your breath as a background reminder to help you witness the past without getting lost.

Let's take the example of getting jilted. Most of us have been rejected at one time or another by someone we desired. In my life, these experiences have been extremely painful. But how does the Soul view such historical events? Contrary to the way the Ego interprets these losses—identifying oneself as the "jilt-ee," the wronged party—the Soul sees a larger dance in motion. Looking back at such painful episodes from this consciousness, we may see that what appeared to be losses in fact led us to happier outcomes. Each of the Ego's "failures" has contributed to making us who we are now. Without meaning to sound saccharine: each step we take in our learning is, from the

Soul's point of view, a blessing. How distant this is from the Ego's harsh judgment, and from our tendency to hold lifelong grudges. There is a lovely poem by Machado de Assis that voices this perfectly:

> Last night as I lay sleeping, I dreamt
> O, marvelous error—
> That there was a beehive here inside my heart
> And the golden bees were making white combs
> And sweet honey from all my failures

The golden bees are the force of the Soul as it reworks experience into wisdom.

This approach to finishing the business of our past can even apply to abuse experiences, difficult as that is to hear. I am not for a moment dismissing the pain of abuse, merely suggesting that we begin to bring our present wisdom to bear on such suffering in the past in order to release its hold upon us. By moving outside the Ego, we can begin to stop identifying with the abuse we've lived through, and to release the fascination we have with our own trauma. We tend to cling to abuse and grievances as signposts of our own identity, and a means to hold onto our past. We become the center of "As the World Turns"; we have the leading role in the play, milking our history as if we need it to justify our existence, to give it meaning. We keep locking ourselves in the prison of our past through fascination with the script.

Just look at it from the point of view of our own consciousness: if we hold grudges, if we don't practice forgiveness, we end up stuck with the old grievances. It is only my attachment to the abuse that makes it my problem, once the actual abuse has stopped. In other words, my mind is perpetuating my own suffering.

Unfortunately, many older people don't seem to realize this. I've spoken to many unhappy individuals who spend a great deal of their time stewing in the memories of wrongs committed toward them in the past. It becomes almost a hobby to tally up the score of offenses, and grind the axe of resentment. This causes only bitterness, though, as I saw in the case of an elderly woman who told me, quite bluntly, that she would never forgive her long-dead parents for the way they'd treated her as a teenager. "Never, as long as I live!" she said with great self-righteousness, pulling her arthritic hands into fists. I was struck by the poignancy and futility of her attitude, which was doing greatest harm to herself. Clearly, she had a choice—to practice forgiveness and letting go, or to stay tethered to this resentment forever.

If you have unresolved business with the dead, it is wise and skillful to find a means of releasing it by bringing mercy and forgiveness into your consciousness. Watch how your mind and body tighten around the memory as it arises, and make an effort, little by little, moment by moment, to soften your heart. There is no need to deny what's happened, to rationalize or justify it in any way, or to negate your own present feelings; rather, your intention is to defuse the pain by acknowledging it fully. Once you start to pay full attention, you see that resentment thrives on subtle resistance; if you are unable to forgive, chances are it's because you don't want to. You may find it helpful to practice forgiveness rituals, such as writing letters to those who have harmed you, or using a photograph to meditate upon, imagining these "enemies" as Souls with their own suffering and ignorance.

As I cultivate an ability to be more and more deeply in the moment, the power of the moment becomes stronger than the memories of the past—even memories of extreme pain. As I move outward from Ego into greater and greater spaciousness, the intensity, the richness, and the fullness of the moment increase.

If we have unresolved business with people who are still alive, I highly recommend meeting them in person. I've changed a lot of relationships, especially with my relatives, by simply sitting down with them and remaining open to something new happening in the relationship. There's no need to be aggressive, to confront them with an ultimatum such as "we need to have a talk!" By simply coming together, you help to bring the past relationship—with all its memories and images of who this person used to be, and what he or she may have done to you—into the present moment. By touching the past with the present, our grievances can begin to dissolve. You may be surprised by how much *energy* such reconciliations release, which tips you off to how much energy you've been spending holding on.

LEARNING TO GRIEVE

It is important, as we get older, to learn how to grieve. Although this may sound self-evident, experience has taught me that it is not. In a culture that emphasizes stoicism and forward movement, in which time is deemed "of the essence," and there is little toleration for slowness, inwardness, and melancholy, grieving—a healthy, necessary aspect of life—is too often overlooked. As we get older, of course, and losses mount, the need for conscious grieving becomes more pronounced. Only by learning how to grieve can we hope to leave the past behind and come into the present moment.

The older we get, the more we lose; this is the law of impermanence. We lose loved ones, cherished dreams, physical strength, work, and relationships. Often, it seems like loss upon loss. All these losses bring up enormous grief that we must be prepared to embrace completely, if we are to live with open hearts.

My dear friend Stephen Levine has recommended that we build temples specifically for the purpose of grieving, ritual sites where we can feel safe to pour out the sadness and loss that we feel. In the Jewish tradition of sitting *shiva*, and in the traditional Irish wake, we find such outlets for extended grieving, but these rituals are becoming rare in our culture and are not frequently practiced.

Over the years, in working with people who are grieving, I've encouraged them first of all to surrender to the experience of their pain. To counteract our natural tendency to turn away from pain, we open to it as fully as possible and allow our hearts to break. We must take enough time to remember our losses—be they friends or loved ones passed away, the death of long-held hopes or dreams, the loss of homes, careers, or countries, or health we may never get back again. Rather than close ourselves to grief, it helps to realize that we only grieve for what we love.

In allowing ourselves to grieve, we learn that the process is not cut and dried. It's more like a spiral that brings us to a place of release, abates for a time, then continues on a deeper level. Often, when grieving, we think that it's over, only to find ourselves swept away by another wave of intense feeling. For this reason, it's important to be patient with the process, and not to be in a hurry to put our grief behind us.

While the crisis stage of grief does pass in its own time— *and each person's grief has its own timetable*—deep feelings don't disappear completely. But ultimately you come to the truth of the adage that "love is stronger than death." I once met with a girl whose boyfriend was killed in Central America. She was grieving and it was paralyzing her life. I characterized it for her this way. "Let's say you're in 'wise-woman training.'" If she's in wise-woman training, everything in her life must be grist for the mill. Her relationship with this man would become part of the wisdom in her. But first she had to see that her relationship with him is between Souls. They no longer have two incarnated bodies to share, so she had to find the Soul connection. Two Souls can access each other without an incarnation.

When my guru died in 1973, I assumed that because of the important part he played in my life, and the love I felt for him, I would be inundated with grief. Surprisingly, I was not. In time, I came to realize why. He and I were so well established in Soul love that, in the years since he left his body, his palpable presence in my life has continued unabated.

SHEDDING ATTACHMENT
TO THE FUTURE

As we learn to come into the present moment, we not only discover that we're able to free ourselves from the past, but from the future as well. As the Tibetan teaching instructs, we learn not to "invite" the future into our thoughts before its time, or to cause ourselves unnecessary discomfort, for just as the past traps us in memories, the future traps us in anticipation.

Confronted by daunting challenges and expectations, many older people spend a great deal of their lives dreading what lies ahead. Although death is certainly our greatest fear, and one we will talk about at length in the next chapter, we also preoccupy ourselves with other concerns that take us away from our current experience and cast us into the sea of what-ifs. This is a futile enterprise; although we must plan for our future by putting our affairs in order, there is nothing to be gained through the sort of obsessive worrying and fretful expectation that characterizes the thinking of many older people.

Most of our fears, if we look at them clearly, relate to how we imagine the future will be. Fear thrives on the unknown, and although many of us avoid what scares us, it is more effective to approach our fears as closely as possible—to bring our *ideas* of the future into the present—in order to disarm them.

Unfortunately, this isn't always a popular strategy. A few years back, I was invited to speak at a benefit for an organization that had been started by an acquaintance of mine who had just died. I knew very few people in the group, but thought that I should do the benefit in my friend's honor. After they suggested a date, I was asked what I wanted to talk about. I told the lady representing the group that I was working on a book about conscious aging, and maybe I could talk about that.

"Oh, I don't think the people of this town would come to a benefit around a subject like aging!" she said.

"Well," I responded, "Maybe I could talk about suffering." She was horrified. They *weren't* interested in suffering.

"I could talk about dying, then—I've been working for years on conscious dying."

"Oh, no! Nobody wants to come to dinner and hear about something like death."

In the end, we agreed that we would call my lecture "Mining the Stages of Life," and I talked about nothing other than aging, suffering, and death. At the end of my lecture, one woman said to me, "You seem very negative. You talk about all these things like getting old and dying." And all the time I thought I was talking about something joyful!

Though we do not wish to "invite" the future, neither can we deny the various possibilities of what may befall us as we age. If we make a list (as I'm prone to do), we realize how unbearable this litany of possible future ills and losses is if we think of ourselves as nothing more than Ego. Without acknowledging the Soul level, or cultivating a Soul consciousness in mindfulness practice, we are like passengers trapped on sinking ships, with no capacity for escape. Once we establish the Soul view, however, we're free to investigate our fears without being smothered by them. As we did in the chapter on the physical body, we may wish to make a list of our worst fears of what may befall us in the future, and reflect upon each one gently, to see how it actually *feels* in the present moment, and so deprive it of power. In her book *This Timeless Moment*, Laura Huxley even offers an exercise for imagining your own funeral. If this is too extreme for you, imagine yourself as I am, in a wheelchair (incapacitation is a common fear about the future), or alone without family or friends. By remaining conscious of the present moment while you contemplate these things, you will see that your thoughts are creating your fear.

TIME AND CHANGE

Time and change are interrelated. We measure time by what changes, and we measure change in increments of time. For many of us, apprehension over what the future may hold is synonymous with our fear of change. As Egos, we resist letting go of the known; change is nearly always viewed as a threat, since the Ego is only comfortable with what it can control. But this is where our conscious aging can help to relieve the anxiety we feel over change: for *the Soul is not subject to change in the same way the Ego is*. It does not measure time in the same way. Soul time is measured in incarnations. Each incarnation is like an hour—or even a minute—to the soul. As the Ego moves in terrestrial time, the Soul exists in Soul time. The Soul thinks in terms of endless eons. By learning to remain in both time perspectives, we experience a stillness that enables us to accept the turbulence of change, and also to catch our breath. Freeing ourselves from the Ego's attachment to things remaining as they are, and acquainting ourselves with what exists eternally in each present moment, we learn to approach change with curiosity rather than dread, and to be more comfortable with "not knowing" than we have been before.

I often tell a wonderful story that illustrates this brand of wisdom. Once, there was a farmer in a village who had a horse that he treasured. One day the horse ran away, and the farmer's neighbor came to his house to offer his condolences. "I'm so sorry for your loss," he said, trying to be a good friend. "You never know," the farmer replied. The very next day, the horse came back, leading a beautiful wild mare alongside him. Again the neighbor piped in: "That's wonderful!" he said. "What a stroke of good luck!" The farmer replied, "You never know." A few days later, the farmer's son was trying to break the wild horse in, was thrown to the ground, and broke his leg. Of course the neighbor came over to say how sorry he was that things had gone badly. The farmer replied, "You never know." A short time later, the Cossack army came through the village in search of young men to fight in the war, but since the farmer's son's leg was broken, he was allowed to stay at home. "Aren't you a fortunate man!" the neighbor said when he heard the news. You can guess what the farmer replied.

The point is that we never know what changes will come, or how they'll affect us. The law of impermanence, *anicca*, requires that if we want to reduce our suffering we learn to weather change as gracefully as possible, remaining open to what we do not know.

A few years ago, I met a fellow named Tom Andrews, who'd run for election as a senator in Maine. Tom had had three bouts with cancer, one of which had cost him a leg. I was impressed by his calm demeanor, and asked him how he managed to remain so cheerful. "After the third time," he said to me, "I finally got the message. I needed to open up to this thing and not live my life in fear. I looked around and found the best treatments, traditional and 'alternative,' then went on with my life. The most important thing is not to dread the future, and to stay open to whatever comes. No matter how strange or new it might be, I just try to tell myself: this is the stuff you're working with now."

So we plan what's plannable, then work with whatever we get. Or as the Marines say, "You change what you can change. And what you can't change, you paint." We acknowledge the fact that as we get older, we're going to lose control (the *Ego* is going to lose control) and we'll be asked to surrender to the unknown in ways we never have before. Since my stroke, I've had to learn this daily, and give over control in ways that have been extremely difficult for someone as strong-willed as I am. But what other choice do we have when we're faced with changes we can't undo? Wisdom requires that we relax our hold on our picture of how things "ought" to be, and learn to make peace with things as they are. We can only do this moment by moment, here and now, by responding with open hearts and minds to the changes that occur.

One of the disquieting things about the changes that come with aging is how our images of ourselves contradict the reality. However much we might feel like teenagers inside, our bodies contradict us at every turn, sometimes—as when I leapt onstage and fell on my face—with painful or embarrassing results. But once again, we discover in this apparently "irreconcilable" problem the seeds of great learning. The older we get, the more likely we are to experience these moments of "cognitive dissonance," when self-image and reality contradict each other. Though this conflict is uncomfortable, it is a clear window into the place where we are clinging, and where we need to pay attention. Just as physical pain alerts us to troubles in the body, mental pain alerts us to where we need to be more conscious. In other words, our frustrations, anger, delusions, and so on become our greatest helpers in freeing ourselves from suffering. They point to where the Ego is trapped, and remind us to begin to shift our identity to the Soul level. They show where we are resisting change, where we are time-bound, and where we need to grow beyond past conditioning.

MOVING TOWARD FEAR

The alternative to accepting change is terrible indeed. We all know people caught in this no-win situation, holding on for dear life to things they cannot control. We see the panic they endure, attempting to hold the future at bay, to keep things exactly as they are, freezing themselves into a rigid and narrow existence. This makes for a kind of half-life—or half-death—in which fear dominates, and traps the fearful man or woman in limbo. Without remaining open to change, we cannot remain open to life; this is the sometimes-frightening truth which we must confront as we get older. The desire to control change is our greatest obstacle to wisdom.

The Ego's relationship to change can be illustrated by looking at the mythology of India, where the Goddess (or life force) is given two primary forms: Kali and Durga. Kali is the frightening Goddess, who wears a garland of skulls around her neck and a belt of severed hands around her waist. Her tongue is dripping blood and she holds a blood-drenched sword. Kali is the Ego's enemy; it is her terrible aspect which we see when we're trying to control the world, or hold on to something. It is Kali's function to crush the Ego and to pry us loose from whatever we're hanging on to.

When we let go of the Ego, Kali becomes transformed into Durga, the golden Goddess, the Great Mother of effulgent radiance. Our curriculum of conscious aging requires that we get as close as possible to Kali, and the thing that's scaring us, in order to reveal our attachments, and to experience the serenity that comes with letting go of them.

Facing dread of the future is an excellent vehicle for entering into the spiritual dimension. *We must be willing to open to all that the moment contains, including that which seems most threatening.* But how do we do this? By cultivating fearlessness, and familiarizing ourselves with our demons.

When I first became involved in work with the dying, my reasons were twofold. First, after spending time with my guru and having metaphysical experiences with him, while on entheogens, and in meditation practice, I imagined that I could bring a helpful perspective to the then-medieval Awareness of death and dying in this country. By sitting *as a Soul* with dying people, most of whom had been raised to believe that they were nothing but their bodies and minds, I hoped to communicate a larger truth, and provide more spaciousness of mind, at a time when it could be most useful.

But my second reason was more personal. I was afraid of dying, as most people are, and wanted to free myself of that fear. I was caught in other struggles as well; aversions, hungers, and confusions that were bound up with my Ego's attachments and ignorance. I needed a crash course in *anicca* to help loosen my bonds. To initiate me more deeply into the law of change and impermanence, I knew that there was no more effective classroom than sitting with people who were confronting death.

Although I'm certainly not free of the fear of death, I can say that sitting with the dying—and consequently with my own aversion—has helped to ease my resistance to death, and to familiarize me with what would otherwise have remained an abstract, and therefore unmanageable, demon. By confronting ourselves consciously and deliberately with mirror reflections of changes that worry or frighten us, we learn to weaken our dread of the future. Having seen the inevitability of change, we are not surprised or overwhelmed when the laws of nature take their course. This does not do away with suffering, but it does cast a different light upon it; unlike the older people I've met who, at eighty or ninety years of age, are still asking "Why me?", we shoulder our burdens with more dignity and good nature, having prepared ourselves for these changes. Change, from the Ego point of view, is suffering. Change, from the Soul point of view, is just change.

In the end, of course, our approach to the future comes down to how we feel about mystery. As much as we may know of ourselves and our existence, there will always be a great deal more that we will never know. The Soul has no trouble with mystery at all. Mystery is the Soul's element. As wise elders, we come to know that the Ego has no control over anything, and so we begin to rest in the mysterious present and let the future unfold as it will.

THE TIMELESS PRESENT

The more we practice conscious aging, the more we come to see how our enslavement to time is a product of our minds. Though you may not be aware of it, you've probably experienced this phenomenon firsthand on many occasions. For example, try to recall how it feels to be utterly absorbed in some activity—reading a good book, say, or making love, or listening to a piece of music that sweeps you up in its beauty—then "snapping to" and realizing that an hour has passed without your knowing it. By focusing your mind on what you're doing (or, perhaps, *unfocusing* it), and stopping the Ping-Pong game of thought that bounces the mind between remembrance and anticipation, you have, for all practical purposes, *fallen out of time*, and freed yourself of past and future. You will notice that after such timeless episodes have passed, your body and mind are in a state of ease and relaxation, as if you've been released from an iron hand that you didn't know was squeezing you. This experience is precisely the aim of conscious aging practices. As we get older and become less active, we can use these techniques to loosen the grip that time holds upon us, and to discover these timeless moments whenever we choose.

The key to this freedom is understanding that *in the present moment, there is no time.* The gospels of the world's great religions make reference to this "eternal present" in their teaching, instructing seekers after God to look no farther than where they're standing for the kingdom of heaven. In other words, *eternity is now,* and by learning to "lose track of time" through present focus, we begin to discover hidden dimensions to everyday experience, which have always been there for us, but have been veiled by our being time-bound. The moment is a doorway into eternity.

We can begin to practice this moment-to-moment Awareness by learning to do one thing at a time. When you are drinking tea, drink tea. When you are reading the paper, read the paper. This helps to slow the mind and stop time-bound patterns. When we attend, with care, to our present activity, we discover a wonderful freedom from thought. In the next sip of tea, the next breath, the next step, no time exists, and with each opportunity you take to come fully into the moment, you'll feel the relief of resting in the eternal present.

This doesn't mean that you won't wear a watch, or follow a schedule, or make plans for tomorrow, but rather that you will be fully attentive to each activity you carry out. With practice, this can steady your mind and decrease anxiety. Though bound by time on a physical level, your Witness will learn to exist outside of it, infusing your "time" with a feeling of timelessness, a present that embraces both the past and the future.

THE THREE FACES OF TIME

Once we begin to understand how "relative" time is, in actuality we start to notice its changing face, like a painted clock by Salvador Dalí, melting into different shapes. We see that there are different kinds of time: the objective tick-tock of Greenwich mean time; the various ways we experience time, which might be called "psychological time"—which drags when we're bored and races when we're happy; and "cultural time," which varies according to a society's accepted pace, the presence or absence of technology, and how time is "defined" (think of "time is money") by any given population.

All three of these aspects of time are relevant to our curriculum for conscious aging. Let's begin with "psychological time." Many older people report that as they age, time seems to move both more rapidly, and more slowly, than ever before. Though the years fly by, the hours drag. There are various explanations for this, beginning with the idea that the older you get, the smaller the fraction a year constitutes in your entire lifespan. In other words, for a ten-year-old, a year is one-tenth of a lifespan, but as we enter our 60s, a year is one-sixtieth of our frame of reference.

Whatever the reason, we recognize that with this perception of time as increasingly brief, we cling to time more tightly the older we get, feeling it slip between our fingers. I frequently hear older people ask, "Where does the time go?" Events that happened ten years before "seem like yesterday." Of course, this disorientation about time can have its positive side, too. My own sense of time has been altered by my stroke, and I'm no longer so trapped by the rigidities of its lock-step patterns. I experience that the more malleable time is for me, the easier it is for me to go through the doorway into the moment.

Just as there are older people for whom time seems to

speed by—keeping them rushing about like rabbits, to and fro, with never enough time to do all they need to do—there are an equal number of older people on whose heads time hangs heavy. Often, they are not very mobile and don't have a great deal of stimulation. This can give rise to feelings of boredom: the sense that time is a kind of torture, like water dripping from a tap. Boredom, in fact, is among the most common complaints of people as they age. But, like so many other experiences, boredom is often not what it seems.

I once went to Myanmar (it was still called Burma at the time) to do a three-month meditation retreat in a monastery. I was given a tiny room with no books or paper, and no one to talk to; nothing to do at all, in fact. Two hours into the three months, sitting there on my meditation cushion, I thought, "I'm bored already." But rather than pushing the thought away, or following it to some conclusion like, "Get me out of here," I decided to examine this boredom more closely. I asked myself, "What does the boredom feel like? Is it square or round? Is it moving or still?" The more I questioned the nature of this boredom from my Soul perspective, the more interesting it became as another set of experiences. Once I got over being worried about being bored, and touched the actual thoughts, images, prejudices, expectations, and physical sensations comprising this state I'd labeled as "boredom," the more I realized that my "boredom" was just an empty idea, and that actually I was merely in another state of consciousness to be explored. This let me see again how full and rich the present moment could be.

As always, attention is the transforming agent.

Beyond "psychological time," we are also subject to "cultural time," which is as endemic to a society as are the language it speaks and the food it eats. As philosopher Ken Wilber has pointed out, ours is not the spiritual age that

New Agers crack it up to be, but rather the Age of Information. It is a culture based on philosophical materialism, and characterized by the rapid pace of our industrialized world.

I was walking behind an elderly couple on Fifth Avenue one day. They were walking very slowly and leaning on each other for support. At a crosswalk, the cars and people were whizzing past trying to catch the changing light. As the couple moved slowly into the crosswalk, I could see how hostile the environment was to these older people. Cars honked at them, people were pushing them to move faster, and they just stood in the crosswalk, confused. They were like Martians in a way, because the fast culture was so different from their pace. I wondered what it would be like if they were living in a small village or town, where there would be people to help them. They would have been more part of the warp and woof of the culture instead of seeming so out of place. I realized the violence done to the spirit of its elderly by our time-obsessed culture.

When my father was close to ninety, I took him for a ride one afternoon to a town called Holliston, outside of Boston. My father's grandfather—the first in our family to come over from Europe—had had a farm out in Holliston when my father was a child, and I had the urge to take Dad back to see the place, for old time's sake. As a boy, my father had lived with his family in a tenement in the North End of Boston, and on weekends they'd take the train out to Holliston. His grandfather would meet them at the station with a horse and buggy and take them to the farm. I thought it would be a pleasant excursion to take Dad back over that route.

I had located the railway station and checked some old maps to find out where the farm had been, and I drove us along an old road to the location. When we got there, we found that the farmhouse was gone, with nothing left but a few decaying boards. At his age, Dad had grown quiet and he hardly said a word, looking around as if he were lost, then staring at the floorboards of the car as we drove away. I was very disappointed! I'd gone to an awful lot of trouble to find out where the farm had been, calling City Hall and such, and put lots of effort into our adventure. Now, he was just ignoring it.

Then suddenly I realized the problem: the whole trip had just passed him by. The day had simply gone too fast! We'd traveled from the station at the speed of an automobile, not the speed of the horse and buggy that Dad remembered. I decided to start over. Back at the railway station, I proceeded slowly toward the farm at the rate that a two-wheeled trap might go with a chestnut mare clip-clopping ahead. And, lo and behold, Dad came alive! Dozens of stories poured out of him. "This is where I fell off the wagon. Here's where we used to get apples!" Dad was full of tales, but it wasn't until we slowed down that his memory was able to come onboard and awaken him to that old place. This helped me to understand why so many old people feel out of step, unable to connect to a world that is moving so rapidly; why, as so many elderly folks have complained to me, they feel that time has left them behind.

While we may accept the new, sometimes the old has to be evoked. Dad was up-to-date, but he was going back into time, into another layer of reality. He wasn't caught in the past, but to get there, he had to move at the pace of his childhood. He didn't lament. Older people often re-experience the time-perspective of childhood—when there wasn't anything pressing to do. I sit on the porch of my house and hang out with my neighbors the trees. I remember that in my childhood I didn't have any busy-ness, just like now. My old age and childhood are both spacious—of time–spacious. This allows the Soul to enter. For Dad, I tried to slow down to recreate the spaciousness he needed to evoke his childhood. The car was being made into a horse and buggy. The car's speed doesn't provide the same spaciousness as does the pace of horse and buggy.

This preoccupation with speed is not only confusing, it is often cruel to older people. I spend a good deal of time in Manhattan, where the pace is a barely controlled mania, and have seen how difficult it is for the old to cope with an urban environment. With the cars whizzing by, and the traffic lights changing too quickly, it's difficult for the elderly to take a walk, or cross a street, without being injured (or feeling like a nuisance, at the least). Watching an older woman maneuver with her cane between taxicabs, whose drivers honked at her to move more quickly, I realized the violence done to the spirit of its elderly by our time-obsessed culture.

Medicine is equally caught in the speed-up. When I was a child, doctors were almost a part of the family, making house calls and stopping for tea. Now, at my health-plan visit, I am happy if the doctor and I have time to shake hands and exchange names within the seven or ten minutes that he has allotted to see me. The same holds true for lawyers. My nephew, who's a lawyer, tells me that he has a special machine hooked up to his telephone to measure every second he spends doing business. Time was, a lawyer didn't bother counting the hours he spent with a client; a lawyer might even share a meal (without charging a fee) with someone whose case he was representing. To our time-bent minds, this now seems romantic—almost hokey—but such was the norm in the not-so-distant past.

SOUL TIME

All the experiences of time we've been talking about—objective time, psychological time, cultural time—are experiences of the Ego. But Soul time is very different. Our Souls live by a different calendar; from the Soul's point of view, our Egos are like mayflies that are born in the morning and die in the evening. As we get comfortable with the Soul's perspective, we shift our relationship to time so that we look at it through the eyes of the Soul.

The more deeply we practice the path of wisdom, and explore the Soul level of our beings, the more aware we become of how little attention our culture pays to sacredness as an aspect of everyday life. Nowhere is this omission more glaring than in the domain of time. We need look no further than the cliché that "time is money" to apprehend how our society views time, or to realize the degree to which secularity pervades our culture's consciousness. We're given to understand that time is something "spent" or "wasted," something we "have" or "don't have," like other material possessions. How rarely do we think of time as sacred, or of the moment as a spiritual gift.

I grew up in a Jewish home, but we didn't observe a weekly holy day. My parents had forgotten the meaning of the Sabbath; we were busy assimilating. Stopping our regular lives on Saturday would have set us apart from our non-Jewish friends.

But something precious was lost in this transition from Old World values to those of this material culture. In the Jewish tradition as in the Christian, the Sabbath is the day when time stops, the day that defines the rest of the week. A few years ago, I was in the ancient Jewish section of Jerusalem over a Sabbath, and was moved by the way the neighborhood stopped, suddenly, at sundown on Friday night. It was as if, as a collective body, the Jews had stopped their worldly commotion in order to take a deep breath together, to reflect, pause, and let go of striving. The Sabbath was a time for meditation, for stopping to pay attention before rushing forward again. For some, of course, keeping the Sabbath is nothing more than a mechanical ritual, a way of being good and respectable people. But for others it is a sacred time reserved to celebrate the mystery of their covenant with God, a time for Souls to be together and make sacred the world they share.

How desperately we need such times of respite and sacredness in our lives as we grow older. Whether we are religious or not, it is helpful to observe a Sabbath, or to think of our meditation practice as a sort of short Sabbath every day. It is necessary to reserve a regular period in which to forget time and busy-ness, and remember the sacred in our lives. Observing a Sabbath helps to bring us into the present moment, replenishing not only our physical and mental energy, but our spirits as well, which require as careful tending as plants in a garden. Taking time out of time nurtures that part of our being which is eternal.

Because I have gone back and forth so often between the United States and India, I have become very sensitized to cultural differences concerning time. One particular memory stands out from 1970, when I was visiting my guru in India after a two-year absence. After traveling at 600 miles an hour on a British Airways 747 from New York via Frankfurt, I was deposited in the middle of the night at the Delhi airport. The moment I stepped out of the plane and smelled the air of India—dust and heat, with a hint of flowers—all notions of speed and efficiency stopped, and a new rhythm began to set in.

Once inside the terminal, we passengers queued up for the long wait at customs, dazed, confused, exhausted, and ornery. It was 3:30 A.M. local time. The line moved so slowly that it seemed not to be moving at all. As Westerners accustomed to speedy service, we were universally annoyed, grumbling and exchanging dirty looks, stamping our feet like impatient children while the agents took their merry time. I'd been through this time-shift before on arrival in India, and knew that my clock-watching mind would have to stop if I didn't want to suffer intolerably, but for the moment I was caught, as miserable as the Westerners around me, while the Indians on line stood stoically nearby.

A few hours later, I was on board the Taj Express train bound for Agra, with a stop at Mathura where I would get off. Traveling by train in India is full of rich lessons. The trains go *slowly*, express or not, and we moved at a prehistoric pace, the countryside creeping by, palm tree by palm tree, until I wanted to open the window and scream. But then something began to shift. Rather than resist the slowness and count the minutes, I told myself a little story. "This trip is going to go on forever," I said inwardly. "This present moment will never end. I've been on this train my entire life, and will never, *ever* get off. Now what?"

Meditating on this story, I began to surrender into the rhythms and speed of the train, looking out the window at the passing images without the anger of moments before. My attention fixed upon a young woman in a field; she was wearing a colorful sari and walking along a path by herself, in one of those middle-of-nowhere places, a large clay jug balanced on her head, her undulating gait allowing her head to remain still as she moved. She was close enough for me to see her eyes, which were underlined with black kohl. She wore a pink hibiscus flower behind her ear and silver bracelets on both wrists.

To my eyes, she was like a Gauguin figure, caught in an action that would never end, her past and future filled in by imagination. As my train moved slowly, purposefully forward, covering the passengers with coal dust, the woman moved more slowly still along a path that extended in both directions, out of sight, seemingly without end. Although she was only in view for half a minute, her existence seemed to penetrate me, forming a profound impression. I was both attracted and repelled—attracted in the part of me that yearned to slow down, to move to the rhythms of earth and sky, the seasonal cycles of planting and harvest, the coming and going of generations; repelled in the part of me raised in the West, accustomed to material life and great stimulation. In that moment, I saw these two aspects in stark relief, and wondered which of these parts was "me."

At the Mathura train station, I found myself accosted by rickshaw *wallas* offering to take me the final six miles of my journey to Vrindaban in their bicycle carriages. If I wanted to move more quickly, I could choose a motorcycle *walla*, or—for five times the price—a taxi that would whisk me to Maharajji in a matter of twenty minutes. Oddly, though, I chose none of these; I longed to remain in the rhythm I'd glimpsed as that woman walked across the field, in order to meet my guru. I settled onto the back floor of a horse-drawn *tonga* for the hour-long trip to the *ashram*.

I arrived with an offering of flowers and fruit, and found myself standing in front of Maharajji. I placed my offerings before him, bowing and smiling, and finally sat on the ground among the others who had come for *darshan* (the Master's blessing). But nothing seemed to be happening! My mind began to charge this way and that, driven by impatience after traveling all that way, but soon it was spinning out of control. I attempted to listen to what was being said, but the teaching seemed trivial to my judging mind. This led to a feeling of mild despair.

I sat with this darkness for a time, then opened my eyes and looked at Maharajji. All of a sudden, time seemed to stop; something about his presence quieted me and brought the moment into focus. He seemed to "fill" time; the dimension of then and now, of coming and going, no longer seemed to apply; in the field of my guru's consciousness, time was no longer a template for measuring experience. The moment was suddenly *enough*—

a word my Western mind could hardly grasp—and there was nothing to look for, to expect or desire, nothing to consume or attain. With time paused, and thinking slowed down, the veil between "me" and the moment fell, bringing a kind of Awareness where past and future melted into now, and there was no boundary. I was no longer Ram Dass, a.k.a. Richard Alpert, jet-set American, who'd just traveled halfway around the world to sit in this place: I was a Soul, as he was a Soul.

I was brought a cup of *chai*—strong, sweet, milk tea—in a small, crudely made clay cup. Later, according to custom, I threw the cup against the wall and watched it shatter onto the ground, to be trampled by cows into dust again. Maharajji asked someone once, "Why are you so prideful? We're all made of clay." Looking at the shards of that cup, in that heightened, timeless moment, I could almost see my own body shattered, already dead, returning to the earth. That thought brought enormous gratitude for the moment of light and breath I was living—how sweet, how rare, to be given a body in which to move about this world! What grace to be alive, and know the day in all its sweetness! Falling out of time this way, coming into the eternal now, I felt a surge of sacred love for everything surrounding me.

Such moments of ecstatic Awareness are not far off and do not require voyages around the world, or the presence of enlightened masters. They are at our fingertips at all times, if we only stop and pay attention to the miracle that dances around us. Being time-bound, we're mostly blinded by what is unfolding every moment; we measure and shrink and define these wonders, but when we stop counting, and open our eyes, a new sort of life awaits us. Though our bodies have aged, the moment is new, and we learn to move in eternal rhythms through the temporal world.

7

LEARNING
TO DIE

Never the Spirit was born—
The Spirit shall cease to be, never.
Never was time it was not—
End and beginning are dreams.
Birthless and deathless and changeless
Abideth the Spirit forever.
Death doth not touch it at all.

THE *BHAGAVAD GITA*

Having come to realize that we are more than the body and mind—and more than their combined self-image, the Ego—we can begin to view dying and death through quite different eyes. We are no longer quite so afraid of our own thoughts and feelings, however disturbing they may be. In learning to step outside the Ego into Soul consciousness, we know that we are more than our thoughts and feelings and the mind that experiences them. We are also Souls, and as such we come to the mystery of dying and death without quite the same level of fear and dread.

I don't mean to sound simplistic. Nor am I implying that I have arrived at a point where death holds no fear for me. Having worked with the dying since the 1960s, I can say without speculation that it is possible to approach our deaths without the degree of emotional suffering that we've come to accept as a given in our culture. I have spent time in India, where the approach to death is radically different than it is in the West. It is possible to prepare ourselves consciously for our own passing-over, and to spend our last days with love in our hearts, and with the kind of support that will help us make this transition. It is possible to meet the moment of death with openness, equipped with our expanded definition of what we human beings are, and to prepare ourselves for what—according to every mystical tradition—will follow after.

MAKING DEATH VISIBLE

Although the work of such pioneers as Cecily Saunders in the hospice movement and Elisabeth Kübler-Ross, Stephen Levine, and Ondrea Levine in their work with death and dying have done a great deal to enlighten us in this area, we remain a society in which death is viewed as the enemy, an onerous "thing" to be hidden or shunned, and separated, physically and philosophically, as much as possible from living. How else would a materialistic culture view the death of our material being except as an abomination and a defeat? This "denial of death," to quote the title of Ernest Becker's groundbreaking book, has created a phobic atmosphere surrounding the issue of our own mortality, as well as the kind of fascination that arises with all taboos. We see this clearly in the culture's obsession with violence, and its preoccupation with such topics as euthanasia, suicide, and casualties of street crime and war. Like anything we seek to repress, the fear of death holds a particular, insidious power over our culture. Underneath our youth-conscious, death-denying veneer, we are, in fact, more morbid than societies in which death is confronted more openly.

This situation was even worse when I was growing up, and it was not until 1961, when I was twenty-nine, that I had witnessed another person's death. To be honest, I'd never wanted to; I was happy for death to stay in the closet where it seemed to belong. But when I began to have spiritual experiences, this apprehension shifted. I experienced a connection with the part of myself that was not the Richard I'd known myself to be, and this awakened me into my Soul consciousness. I realized first-hand that although my Ego was certainly going to die one day, and Richard would no longer exist, my Soul would continue its evolution in another form.

When I was in my 30s, my mother was diagnosed with a terminal blood disorder. I went to visit her in the hospital, and all the people around her were saying things like, "You look great!" "You'll be home in no time!" But she looked terrible, and it was likely she'd never come home again. No one—not my father, her sister or the rabbi—would tell her the truth. In that moment I saw just how isolated she was. She was dying and no one would talk to her about death. We spoke about it, Soul to Soul, and she began to relax. This is one of the things that inspired me to begin working with dying people.

Since that time, my entire attitude toward death has changed, and the implications for my life have been profound. Though I'm not completely rid of fear—no one short of a liberated being, of whom there are very few, can claim this—I can honestly say that from where I sit today, death does not terrify me as it did; on a good day, with my mind at peace, death and life seem almost equally appealing. Thanks in large part to this stroke, which has brought death a great deal closer, I've learned to relax my hold on this body, to rest in life—as a wonderful woman saint put it—like a bird resting on a dry branch, ready to fly away.

Just as every spiritual tradition offers its own version of the afterlife, they all agree that preparation for death is the single most important spiritual practice available to us throughout our lives. In confronting our own extinction, we are forced to ask ourselves the question: is there something beyond this body, and if so, what is it? Without death, we would have no choice but to live our lives in ignorance. Death is the wake-up call, the unavoidable mandate, that makes enlightenment possible, and helps our Souls to grow. This is why Plato, when asked on his deathbed for one final word of advice, responded to his pupils, "Practice dying." Death is the final stage of our healing, to bring us closer still to God.

In the thirty years since I sat with my first dying friend, I've sought out every opportunity to be with people at the time of their deaths. Reflecting on these hundreds of experiences, I've come to see that there are three root questions surrounding death for most of the people I've met:

1. How do I deal with the processes of dying?
2. What happens to me at the moment of death?
3. What will happen to me after I die?

Whether people are facing death themselves, confronting the death of a loved one, or working professionally with the dying, their concerns seems to center on the same three questions. There are some who say that they can handle the dying part, but don't like the idea of being dead. Others seem quite prepared to be dead if only they didn't have to endure the dying. (This reminds me of Woody Allen's quip: "I don't mind dying. I just don't want to be there when it happens.") Finally, there is fear of the death moment itself, that we may find ourselves in the wrong place or state of mind to meet the end peacefully.

There is a Sufi story that touches on this last fear. Walking along the street in his village, a man sees Death coming toward him, and is shaken when Death reacts with a look of surprise. Interpreting this look to mean that Death has come for him, the man flees to another village as fast as he can. Once there, however, he meets Death again. This time, Death takes him by the arm and says, "Come."

The man says, "But Death, I saw you in the other village looking at me strangely, so I fled here."

Death replies, "Indeed, I was surprised to see you in your village. But that is because I knew I was to pick you up here in such a short time."

And then there is the Zen student who queried his master as to what happens after. His master smiled and said, "I do not know."

"How can that be? You are a Zen Master."

"Yes," he replied. "But I am not a dead Zen Master."

In other words, examining death will not necessarily give us answers. By beginning to ask the important questions, however, we instigate a process of opening and deepening that can alter our lives in miraculous ways by bringing the Awareness of impermanence and death into the present moment. Though I feel blessed for the years I've spent with the dying, and better prepared to meet my own end, I haven't arrived at any conclusions, knowing that each person's death is different and contains a mystery that cannot be fathomed. "Be patient," Rilke advised, "with all that is unresolved in your heart, and try to love the questions themselves. Do not seek for the answers that cannot be given, for you wouldn't be able to live with them, and the point is to live everything. Live the questions now, and perhaps without knowing it, you will live along someday into the answers."

WHAT HAPPENS AFTER DEATH?

What happens after we die? Though I have no experience of this realm myself, I've come to believe that some part of us does indeed endure the death of the physical body, given the wealth of evidence from spiritual traditions, and the personal testimony of near-death survivors. But what it is precisely that endures remains a mystery. A Laotian Buddhist master answered the question of what remains after death by saying: "Truth remains." When the great Hindu Master Ramana Maharshi was dying, he replied to his devotees' frantic pleas not to leave them by saying, "But where would I go?" As one of my great Tibetan Buddhist teachers, Kalu Rinpoche, once put it:

We live in illusion, the appearance of things.
But there is a reality. We are that reality.
When you understand this you see that you
are nothing,
and being nothing, you are everything. That is all.

Although such utterances, delivered from the level of Absolute Awareness, seem fairly incontestable, we ask ourselves nevertheless whether we, *personally*, will exist after our own deaths. The answer to this question depends on who—or rather, what—we take ourselves to be. If we subscribe to a materialistic view of things, and believe ourselves to be nothing more than our body and Ego, the answer is almost certainly no. Richard Alpert, a.k.a. Ram Dass, will cease to be when this body has stopped breathing. But if we have expanded our consciousness to include the Soul and Awareness levels, we understand that the physical organism is merely the shell, the rented apartment. Knowing myself to be a Soul, I realize that something will indeed survive death, though this body and personality will be gone.

Anyone who has visited the Indian subcontinent knows how strong the cultural identification with the Soul remains there, despite the effects of modernization. In India, life is seen as a single chapter in a book, not the entire tome; death is viewed as a transformative experience, not the end. As such, there isn't the same fear of death that we suffer from in the West. When a Hindu dies, he or she is wrapped in a sheet, placed on a pallet, and then carried through the streets to the cremation ground. The procession chants, "*Satya Hey, Satya Hah*"—God is Truth. Death is public, for everybody to see—the body is right there, not hidden in a box. Finally, the body is burned by the river, with the family present. During the ceremony the elder son uses a stick to crack open his father's skull before it explodes in the flames.

Most people in India die at home, surrounded by family. Thus, from childhood on, most Indians have been in the presence of death—or, as they put it, "dropping the body," which the Soul no longer needs. The more conscious the individual, the more conscious the death, and what will follow. Those great saints who have attained Pure Awareness are able to drop the body with no fuss at all, realizing that—in the larger scheme of things—little is actually happening. One such saint, Anandamayi Ma, gave a glimpse of what existing at this level of consciousness is like when she responded to a question about who she was.

> "Father, there is little to tell. My consciousness has never associated itself with this temporary body. Before I came on this earth, father, I was the same. I

grew into womanhood, but still, I was the same. When the family in which I had been born made arrangements to have this body married, I was the same. And father, in front of you now, I am the same. And even afterwards, though the dance of creation changes around me in the hall of eternity, I shall be the same."

To spend time in India is to learn by osmosis; surrounded by hundreds of millions of people who look at the death of the body and the continuity of the Soul in this expanded way, I found my own beliefs strengthened.

There are only a handful of people alive who can claim firsthand knowledge of this level of consciousness, and yet it does point to a potential we all share, the potential to identify with the part of ourselves that transcends our body, mind, and even our Soul, and finds refuge in the Nameless essence that cannot be destroyed by death.

So as not to romanticize the East, it is important to note that a great many Western philosophers and thinkers have, at some moment in their lives, seen through the veil of death and written about what comes afterward. A few examples:

"Death is nothing more than a migration of the soul from this place to another."

—Plato

"Do you see, oh my brothers and sisters, it is not chaos and death. It is form and union and plan. It is eternal life. It is happiness."

—Emerson

"What happens after death is so unspeakably glorious that our imaginations and our feelings do not suffice to form even an approximate conception of it."

—Jung, after his 1944 heart attack

"I am just as certain as you see me here that I have existed a thousand times before, and I hope to return a thousand times more."

—Goethe

"After all, it is no more surprising to me to be born twice than it is to be born once."

—Voltaire

What happens after death is a central theme of all the world's religions, rooted as they are in a mystical view of the individual. This is not to say that the conclusion reached by these diverse religions is the same, however. Each culture interprets the after-death experience according to its own dominating images, and the mythology of its own religion. We can take the story of the blind men and the elephant as a metaphor for these cultural differences. Confronted by the enormous beast, several blind men touch him in different places and fall to arguing. "The elephant is like a tree," says the one who is holding a leg. "No, no, he's much more like a wall!" insists the one who is touching the elephant's side. "A rope!" says the one who is holding the trunk, and so the bickering continues, though the blind men are touching the very same creature.

So it is with all mystical experience, including descriptions of the afterlife. Every attempt to describe what happens after we die—the *bardos* in the Tibetan texts, the mansions in the Kabbala, the heaven and hell of Christianity, the ground of being in Buddhism—point to the same thing: that is, a realm that the Soul enters after death. Mystical texts frequently use the image of a finger pointing at the moon to describe our efforts to articulate metaphysical reality, the finger representing the words and images we employ to make symbols for what is beyond our grasp. In this same way, though we cannot capture the after-death experience in language, we can point convincingly toward the fact that some form of afterlife does exist. The mind cannot know what is beyond the mind, and death is the dividing line between these levels of reality.

Having learned to step outside our Egos and observe reality from the Soul's perspective, we have already prepared ourselves to reflect on this mystery of the afterlife while we are in a body. Although this may sound futile or contradictory, it is not—provided we open our minds to what we do not understand. Rilke put this beautifully when he wrote "That one can contain death, the whole of death . . . can hold it in one's heart gentle, and not refuse to go on living, is inexpressible." And yet, by allowing the mystery of death, and what comes after, to *inform* our everyday lives, we begin to see things anew. We begin to ask ourselves new questions. If death is not the end, we might wonder, how should that affect how I live today? How does this open-ended proposition alter my expectations, fears, grief, or solace? There is, after all, a pleasure to be found in the notion that everything ends in death—a nihilist pleasure, perhaps, but comforting nonetheless to the sort of person who likes finite answers, and for whom the prospect of continuing beyond the body and mind he or she knows is more frightening than ending in dust. If karma and reincarnation truly exist, do we live more conscientiously now, aware that our actions will affect our rebirth, or do we become complacent (as one sees all too often in the East) in the belief that we have aeons ahead of us to work out the kinks in our character, and lifetimes in which to achieve our goals?

These sorts of questions can easily become a parlor game if we miss their relevance to our present lives. Reincarnation is an excellent example. If one subscribes to a mystical view of existence, there seems to be little doubt that rebirth does, in fact, occur. But what does this matter to us, the living? If we are trying to learn to live in the present moment, what value can there possibly be in contemplating some future existence or, for those drawn to past-life exploration, the details of who we have been in the past? The answer is fairly obvious. By realizing that our present actions affect not only the world around us, but a Soul consciousness that goes on after we've died, the imperative to wake up now—and live as wisely as possible today—becomes that much more vivid.

It is widely believed that the state of our consciousness at the moment of death affects the trajectory of our reincarnation. Whether we believe in reincarnation or not, we can use this concept by aspiring to be as peaceful, compassionate, and wise as possible when we come to the end. Then, if this mystical interpretation is true, and our Souls are given future births according to how we've lived, we will have done well in the large scheme of things; and if we do not reincarnate, we will at least have lived, and died, in a worthy manner. That said, it is important that we not become judgmental of our own dying process, or fearful when we lapse in mindfulness, courage, or compassion. I have met several well-meaning people engaged in the dying process who added to their burden of suffering by fearing that they were too ignorant to die as they were, believing that they (or their Souls) would suffer afterward in hell, or in some lowly incarnation. Such feelings are not helpful as we come to face the greatest challenge of our lives, nor are they quite accurate. It is the Ego, after all, that strives so hard to do things "right," and that fantasizes about our auspicious future births. Though we can change our consciousness, and thus alter the quality of our death, we do not determine our own reincarnation. This process occurs in Soul time, which the Ego can never fathom. There is a story about the Buddha being asked how long he had been incarnating. He answered, "Consider a mountain the length and width and height that a water buffalo can walk in one day. Now imagine a bird with a silk scarf in its beak that flies across the mountain once every hundred years, letting the scarf brush across the mountain top. In the length of time that it would take for the scarf to wear away the mountain—that is how long I have been incarnating."

While reincarnation remains a controversial topic in a Judeo–Christian culture (references to reincarnation were deleted from the Bible at the Councils of Trent, Nicea, and Constantinople between A.D. 300 and 600), the possibility of rebirth has gained credibility in the West in recent years. Many people I've spoken to have reported uncanny experiences of contact with loved ones who have died. A few years back, my own atheistic family was touched by such an unusual occurrence. My Mother and Dad used to exchange one red rose on every anniversary as tokens of their love. After Mother died, there was a large funeral service at the temple, with many relatives and friends there to share the grief. The casket was covered with a blanket of red roses; as the casket was wheeled down the aisle past the first row in which my father (a very practical lawyer) and the rest of the family were seated, one red rose fell off the blanket and landed at my father's feet. As we were leaving, my father reached down and picked up the rose. In the limousine, when someone suggested that perhaps the rose was a message from Mother from beyond the grave, everybody agreed—even my father. In the passion of the moment, my very down-to-earth family accepted a "miracle."

Of course the next thought in the car was, "How will we save the rose?" Immediately after the funeral, there was a flurry of inquiries and phone calls, and a few days later the rose was nested in an iced container and taken to the airport to be transported to another city for the preservation process. It came back sealed in liquid in a glass globe, and Dad put it on the mantelpiece. Sadly, the method of preservation didn't work very well, and slowly the liquid turned brackish; after a few years, when Dad was ready to remarry, Mother's last message had become an embarrassment, and ended up in the back of the garage, where I found it and put it on my holy table, as a reminder of *anicca*, the impermanent nature of physical life.

Since I do believe that Souls exist after death, I encourage people who are grieving the loss of loved ones to speak to the Souls of those who have passed. This is consoling and, I believe, helpful to both the living and the dead, who are often confused about where they are, and whether (and how) to move on. Since most of us live our lives strictly identified with our Egos, our personalities, and our own bodies, death may be our first conscious contact with our own Souls, and may leave us feeling rather lost. In traditions such as Tibetan Buddhism, specific practices have been developed to help the Soul in this after-time to move through the bardos toward its next incarnation. In our own way, we can aid this process by holding the Soul of the dead one in our hearts.

THE MOMENT OF DEATH

The moment of death is the veil between the dying person and the afterlife. If the experience of death is in any way parallel to the mystical experiences I have had, which entailed a temporary dissolution of the Ego structures, it seems reasonable to expect, at the moment of death, a dissolution of the conceptual map by which we have charted reality. This dissolution is likely to begin slowly and then accelerate, culminating in the final discontinuous experience of passing through a barrier into the Soul dimension.

Naturally, we wish to meet the moment of death as consciously as we possibly can. We wish to die calmly, peacefully, filled with joy, love, and a sense of grace—not to mention a certain excitement regarding the adventure that lies ahead. My friend, the poet Allen Ginsberg, felt this way when he was dying. During his last days, he told his friends that he was "having a ball."

Many who have experienced near-death experiences are often left with excitement—going toward warmth, love, light, reunion with relatives. Their taste of death is a good one. My first taste was a difficult one. In 1963 I was swimming in the ocean one night in Mexico while on acid. My mind was clear and the night was spectacular, so much so that I began to become disoriented by the lights reflected in the water. The waves were big, and I was right in them, and knew that if I was pulled under by one, I might not be able to resurface because I didn't know which way was up or down. I wasn't sure whether or not I was going to come out of this one. As I faced what I thought was my own death, all I could think about were the social ripples of that death. Close friends would come together to grieve, time would pass, and I would only live in other people's minds. The memory of me would fade, until one day a little girl might ask her mother, "Who was Richard Alpert?" I didn't think of my own process, just what other people would think when I was gone.

The acid I had taken changed me in that moment. I discovered that my consciousness could withstand a change of venue. I would survive. I could go into those acid trips not knowing the outcome, but I did learn that no matter what happened—no matter how many misconceptions were blown apart, no matter how many terrifying things came up—even with nothing to hold on to, I would surrender and survive. I was able to learn this and rely on this fact over and over again. When you've felt enough ecstasy, you're not going to cling to structure. Part of fear of death is clinging to structures like Ego.

In those acid trips, and in meditation, I experienced the fact that the Soul is not located in my body, nor is it limited to my body. Though the body dies, I know that Awareness goes on. I now think my death will be like an acid trip with my guru at the end. I'll go through some wild experiences, and then he'll be there waiting. I don't think that it will be traumatic, because my guru and I are Soul-connected. Faith and devotion are strong enough to override the fear. This isn't just something I believe, I came to know it on a visceral level. You have to find that experience yourself. You will know that you are not just material. You will know that death is just the rapids at a bend in the river, and right now we can't see around the corner.

The moment of death does not necessarily transform us; we die, after all, as who we are, no better or worse, no wiser or more ignorant. We each bring to the moment of our passing the summation of all that we've lived and done, which is why we must begin as soon as possible to prepare ourselves for this occasion by waking up, completing our business, and becoming the sort of people who can close their eyes for the last time without regrets. Since none of us knows when the time of death will come, we practice moment-to-moment Awareness. Sitting in meditation, we watch our breath moving in and out of our bodies, aware of how fragile this breath is, and how easily it could stop. Rather than making us fearful, this knowledge keeps us alert and sensitive.

In learning to meet the moment of death with open eyes, and open hearts, it is instructive to look at how great beings have met theirs. After Gandhi was shot at close range while walking across his garden, he died with the name of "Ram" on his lips because he'd spent a lifetime repeating God's name. My own guru, Neem Karoli Baba, uttered *"Om Jai Jagdish Hare"* (Honor to the One who makes the world turn) just as he was dying. As a Japanese Zen Master approached death, reminded that he had yet to compose his death poem, he picked up his pen and scribbled, "Birth is thus. Death is thus. Verse or no verse, what's the fuss?" He died only moments later.

My stepmother Phyllis, just as she was about to die, said, "Richard, sit me up." I did as she asked, putting one hand on her chest to keep her from falling forward, one hand on her back to keep her from falling backward, and my head against her head to keep it from rolling. Then Phyllis took three long, slow breaths and died. This is just the way the great Tibetan masters have always done it—sitting up, three long breaths, then they're gone. How did she know? Not everyone dies in so easy a manner. When he was at the end, the cantankerous founder of Gestalt therapy, Fritz Perls, was giving his nurse a hard time. "Please lie down, Dr. Perls, you shouldn't be sitting up," she begged. To which he replied, "Nobody tells Fritz Perls what to do," and died. My friend Tim Leary's last words are purported to be, "Why? Why not?"

There is a superb story from a bygone era about an army officer and a monk that suggests how a conscious being might meet the moment of death. Once upon a time there was a conquering army going through villages, killing and pillaging as it went. The soldiers caused terror in the hearts of the people in the countryside, and were especially harsh with the monks they found in the monasteries, not only humiliating them but often subjecting them to terrible physical torture.

There was one particularly harsh army captain who was infamous for his cruelty, and when he arrived in a certain town, he asked his adjutant for a report about the people who lived there. His inferior reported: "All the people are very frightened of you and are bowing down to you." This gave the captain great pleasure, of course. Then the adjutant continued, "In the local monastery all the monks have fled to the mountains in terror. Except for one monk."

Hearing this, the captain became furious and rushed to the monastery in search of the monk who dared to defy him. When he pushed open the gates, there in the middle of the courtyard stood the monk, watching him without fear. The captain walked up to him and asked in his haughtiest voice, "Don't you know who I am? Why, I could take my sword and run it through your belly without blinking an eye!"

"And don't you know who I am?" replied the monk, gently. "I could have your sword run through my belly without blinking an eye." It is said that the captain, recognizing the greater truth of the moment, sheathed his sword, bowed, and left.

It is fair to say that what worries us today will worry us on our deathbeds. Since dying is often not easy, it will be helpful to have as much equanimity and clarity as possible to meet this challenge and reduce our suffering. In his book *How We Die*, Sherwin Nuland describes the physical and emotional distress that come at the moment of death, the stoppage of circulation and starving of the heart muscle (upsetting its natural rhythm and forcing it into "the chaotic squirming of ventricular fibrillation"), the inadequate transport of oxygen to tissues, the failure of organs, and the destruction of vital centers. With these can come the experiences of constriction or a viselike grip in the chest, a cold sweat, shortness of breath, perhaps vomiting, and often excruciating pain. The question is, Where can we hope to stand in our own consciousness during such traumatic conditions, in order to die with clarity and grace?

The answer is, in our Soul consciousness. To the degree that it is possible, we wish to be able to stand aside from the death of the body and view this transition from Awareness. This is extremely difficult but not impossible, as the testimonies of conscious beings prove; in any case, we aspire in that direction, knowing that the degree to which we can enter Soul consciousness at the time of our deaths will stabilize us through the tumult of dying. With this in mind, our mindfulness practice takes on new importance. Just as an athlete prepares for a contest by strengthening his or her muscles, we prepare for death by balancing our minds, and easing our access to Witness consciousness.

The more we are helped in this process, the better. Just as we employ midwives to help an infant in its birth, we would be wise in this culture to employ individuals specially trained to help us die. It is tragic, but true, that most people die alone in our culture, in hospital beds in the middle of the night. This is not unlike pushing a boat out to sea at night without a map or light or compass, and no word of advice for the lone sailor. How different this is from the way of traditional spiritual cultures! In Tibetan practice, for example, monks and nuns are instructed in ways to guide the dying through their transition. They are trained to deal with the dying person's thirst, coldness, heaviness, and breathlessness, encouraging the one who is dying not to cling to these phenomena. They offer such instructions as these: "As the earth element leaves, your body will feel heavy. As the water element leaves, you will feel dryness. As the fire element leaves, you may feel cold. As the air element leaves, your outbreath will be longer than your inbreath. The signs are now here. Don't get lost in the detail. Don't cling to any of these phenomena. They are part of a natural process. Let your Awareness go free."

We can transform ourselves into beings capable of meeting these phenomena consciously and without resistance. Although this final life situation may differ in intensity from other experiences we've had, the preparation is the same; namely, learning to meet each thought and sensation as it arises with an open, loving heart, not clinging to the experience through either attraction or aversion, and bringing ourselves back to clear Awareness. I find it delightful that the optimal way I can live my life from moment to moment is also the optimal way I can prepare for my death, and equally delightful that acknowledging our future death is a prerequisite for living a truly joyful life now. Keeping death present in our consciousness, as a great mystery and opportunity for transformation, imbues this moment with a richness and energy that denial saps. Confucius once advised that "Those who find the way in the morning can gladly die in the evening." Although this paradox may appear daunting, it is, when viewed from the Soul perspective, a tremendous blessing.

Sometime during the Eighties, while listening to radio station WBAI in New York, I heard an interview with Pat Rodegast, who was in contact with a disembodied being named Emmanuel. There was something very simple and direct about the things that Emmanuel said "through" Pat, and some time later, I was introduced to Pat through a close friend of mine. I asked him, "Emmanuel, I deal a lot with the fear of death in many people. What should I tell people about the moment of death?" He answered, "Ram Dass, tell them that death is *ab-*

solutely safe." And then he added, "It's like taking off a tight shoe." This corroborated my own suspicions from what I'd seen among dying people, and in my own mystical journeys.

PREPARING FOR DEATH

We come now to the third root fear: How do we prepare for death? Mindfulness and meditation are great ways to stabilize the mind and heart, and for readying ourselves for this challenge. But the moment of death can be truly scary. Let's use the analogy of white-water rafting to look more deeply at this question. In order to ride the most powerful white-water rapids, professionals rigorously train themselves not to lose their cool in the midst of rocks and torrents and waterfalls. It is one thing to imagine dying and another to be faced with "Hey, I'm going right now," and remain calm in that moment. To face such rapids with clarity, one must be acquainted with how water (impermanence) feels, to "keep death present on one shoulder" always, as Carlos Castaneda's teacher Don Juan advised him to do. The wisdom of remembering death, and preparing for it in each moment, may be figurative—as in the dropping of autumn leaves—or literal, as on a gravestone I found in New England, that read:

Dear friend, please know as you pass by,
As you are now, so once was I.
As I am now, so you will be.
Prepare yourself to follow me.

There is a common misconception that preparing for death will diminish the quality of our lives, but this is not the case. In my work with the dying, I've found consistently that the time I spend in the presence of people on their deathbeds is the time when I feel most profoundly alive. Marcel Proust, that great observer of the human comedy, remarked along these same lines when he was asked in a newspaper questionnaire how people would behave in a worldwide disaster promising imminent, certain death:

> I think that life would suddenly seem wonderful to us if we were threatened to die as you say. Just think of how many projects, travels, love affairs, studies, it—our life—hides from us, made invisible by our laziness which, certain of a future, delays them incessantly.
>
> But let all this threaten to become impossible forever, how beautiful it would become again! Ah! If only the cataclysm doesn't happen this time, we won't miss visiting the new galleries of the Louvre, throwing ourselves at the feet of Miss X, making a trip to India.
>
> The cataclysm doesn't happen, we don't do any of it, because we find ourselves back in the heart of normal life, where negligence deadens desire. And yet we shouldn't need the cataclysm to love life today. It would have been enough to think that we are humans, and that death may come this evening.

As Proust implies, keeping death at arm's length prevents us from embracing our lives as fully as we would with mortality closer in our consciousness. With both death and love, it is the dissolving of boundaries between ourselves and the mystery that loosens the hold of the Ego and allows the Soul to be revealed.

In my own life, this effort to accept the gift of death has been rigorous and deliberate. It has been a training of the mind and heart, to identify with the candle of truth, and of attention, until it doesn't flicker even in situations of great turmoil. To make myself light enough to meet this mystery wisely, I've had to throw a lot of stuff overboard. I've had to complete business with people both living and dead. It is not important that we actually address the person with whom we are entangled, but rather that we release whatever holding we may have in our heart surrounding our relationship with that person. We ask ourselves a vital question: do we wish to die with this trouble in our consciousness? Almost always, the answer is no. Death has a marvelous way of throwing the Ego-related dramas into their proper perspective. Very few problems are worth carrying into the moment of our death, and by doing a thorough inventory of where we remain stuck, we prepare the way for a peaceful passing.

Besides completing our work with other people, it is also important that our affairs be in order, legally, medically and financially. It is advisable to sign a "living will," releasing your medical caregivers from the responsibility for keeping your body alive at any cost if you don't want them to, and to donate your organs to medical research should they prove to be viable if you would like to make that kind of contribution. Additionally, we should specify in writing how we wish our bodies to be handled when we die. Where do we wish to buried, or do we wish to be cremated? It is also helpful to talk these details over with those who will be responsible for executing our wishes, as we learned when an aunt of mine died. My father's baby sister was a feisty, rebellious sort of lady, who—after being diagnosed with a brain tumor in her 60s—insisted that she be cremated, which runs counter to the laws of Judaism. After she died and her wishes had been carried out, the family wanted to place her ashes in the family plot, but cemetery administration would have none of it—after all, it was a Jewish cemetery. This created a serious dilemma, and late one night, my uncle and aunt, with torch, shovel, and urn in hand, climbed over the cemetery wall, dug a little hole in the family plot, interred her ashes, hid the incriminating evidence, and fled. Although they weren't caught, this could have been a legal disaster.

Making up a will is difficult for some people. There's a superstitious belief that as long as the will has not been done, they can't die—a kind of magical thinking that can lead to confusion and trouble for those whom we leave behind. As a lawyer, my father spoke often about families and friendships being ripped apart over estate litigation. It is our responsibility to care as well as we possibly can for those who remain when we're gone. This attention to our material affairs is part of our spiritual practice—symbolizing, as it does, the final relinquishing of worldly power.

Important, too, is our choice of where we wish to die. In preparing for our own passing, this is one of the most crucial decisions we need to make—before the advent of a crisis, if possible. Do we wish to be in a hospital where access to medical intervention is the high priority, or would we prefer to be at home? How can we bring a spiritual atmosphere into the place where we die, to render our passing more soulful, and help us to remain conscious? In Japanese Pure Land Buddhism, for example, it is customary to place a screen portraying the heavenly abode at the foot of the bed (in place of something like family photographs) to enable the dying person to focus on where he or she is going, rather than on where he or she has been. My mother's was a typical Western death. For the ten years of her illness—her rare blood disorder ended up turning into leukemia—she was a research subject at the benevolent Dr. Gardiner's blood labs at the Brigham Hospital in Boston.

Dr. Gardiner became one of our family deities, with Mother trying so hard to please him, and to be a good "research subject." Although she passed away more than thirty years ago, it still pains me to think of the environment in which she died. Mother was surrounded in the hospital by people who were saying things like "Gert, you're looking better," and "The doctor has a new medicine for you—you'll be up and around in no time." Afterward, these same people would go out into the corridor and say, "She's looking terrible, she *can't* last much longer." The doctors, the nursing staff, the relatives—all of them seemed to be involved in this deception and denial. Nobody seemed to want to share the truth with her. Mother and I sat together watching this procession of deceit pass through her room. When we were finally alone, she said, "You know, Rich, I think I'm going to die." And I said, "I think you are, too." Then she asked, "What do you think death's like?" We talked about that awhile, and I said to her, "You feel to me like somebody in a building that's collapsing. But our connection seems to be independent of the building. You'll go on even though your body won't. And we'll stay connected." She said that that was how she felt as well. We were in that space together just long enough to recognize it; only a moment, but there was a lot of solace for both of us in being together in that way.

Mother begged the doctors to allow her to return home from the hospital. She wanted to be in her own room again. Finally, they gave their reluctant approval, and she was brought home by ambulance. It seemed pretty obvious that after a ten-year struggle with her disease, she was now going to die. I was visiting her for one last time, and needed to fly to California to give a lecture at the Santa Monica Civic Center that weekend. Although I didn't expect to see her again, fulfilling my lecture engagement seemed more compelling to me at that moment than being with her when she passed away. This is not a choice I would make today, but I was young and ambitious, and have had to live with this decision ever since.

After Mother had spent a day at home, the doctors decided that she was too sick to stay there, and arranged to take her back to the hospital, in spite of her pleas to be left at home. My father, who was very uneasy about death, supported their professional opinion, believing that "the doctors know best." I knew that this was not true, and that Mother should be allowed to die where she felt most comfortable, but I felt intimidated by the majority rule, and by a set of values I did not adhere to. So I remained quiet. Mother was moved back to the hospital and the next night she died alone in an ICU cubicle full of machines, cut off from her grandchildren, who weren't allowed to enter there, and from her beloved home.

Since the time of my mother's death, the hospice movement has made its appearance in this country. Hospice offers a welcome alternative to dying in a hospital for people whose illness, or lack of care, makes it impossible for them to die at home. Underlying the hospice movement is a far more enlightened view of dying: as a natural process not to be interfered with beyond a certain point. For those of us wishing to approach death consciously, hospice may be an excellent environment, relieved of the medical imperative to keep the body alive at any cost. There are also many caregivers within the hospice program who are deeply appreciative and supportive of the spiritual significance of the dying process.

This is not to vilify doctors and hospitals: great good is done every day by medical professionals who, for the most part, are dedicated to the profoundly spiritual ideal of relieving suffering. What's more, many hospitals have relaxed their policies regarding patient autonomy. In the 1970s, just a decade after my mother's death, I was sharing time with Debbie Matthiessen, the wife of the writer Peter Matthiessen. Debbie was dying of cancer in one of the pavilions at Mt. Sinai Hospital in New York City. She was associated with a Zen center in New York, and the monks had begun to come to her hospital room to meditate and help her prepare for the moment of passing. They created a small shrine in one of the corners of the room, and when they began to chant, the hospital room was transformed into a tiny temple. One day, while the monks were there, the hospital physicians making their rounds came barging in with their clipboards, stethoscopes, and professional cheeriness, asking as they entered, "How are we doing today?" The spiritual atmosphere of the room was so strong, however, that the doctors were stopped in their tracks, fell silent in midsentence, and retreated quickly in disarray! Debbie had succeeded in creating a sacred space in which to drop her body, and not even the force of those crisp white coats could affect it.

Although dying at home, surrounded by what is familiar to us, can be deeply reassuring, it can sometimes make leaving more difficult. The presence of beloved objects and people exerts a force that can interfere with the dying process. Meaning no harm, our loved ones wish us to remain among them, even as Nature is pulling us away. This can create a terrible battle in the heart of the dying person, whose Soul wishes to move on, but whose Ego clings to life. We must be aware of this danger during our own deaths and the deaths of people we love. I was told about a twenty-eight-year-old woman named Michelle, who was dying of cancer in a hospital, and whose mother, a nurse in that very hospital, was working triple-time to keep her only child alive, sleeping in the next bed, leaving her side only to use the bathroom. During one of these lavatory breaks, Michelle whispered to another nurse, "Please tell my Mom to let me go." This wasn't possible, however, and it was not until her mother was persuaded to go out to dinner one night that Michelle managed to slip away.

Besides choosing where we want to die, it is important to establish how conscious we want to be at the moment of death. There are, of course, so many unexpected things that happen around death that it is difficult to predict exactly what will happen, or what will be necessary, when the time comes, but we can let our preferences be known. This is not a simple issue. Although pain management has made enormous strides in the past twenty years, it remains a slippery slope. Since most doctors are concerned solely with the body, and place little emphasis on the quality of the dying person's consciousness, we ourselves must try to determine how much of the suffering we see on the deathbed is due to the patient's struggle to remain conscious against the onslaught of narcotizing drugs. In their zeal to alleviate one kind of suffering, are doctors helping to create another by overlooking the importance of meeting our deaths with open eyes? As an advocate of conscious aging, and conscious death, I tend to think that this is the case. In a medical establishment built on a materialistic model, practitioners are bound to focus their attention on what they can see, feel, and measure. Believing, as most do, that the death of their patients' bodies signifies the tail end of those patients' existence, doctors pay little attention to dying and death as phenomena unto themselves, with bearing on future incarnation. Committed to a Soul-centered view of ourselves, we cannot trust medical doctors, therefore, to safeguard our consciousness at the end.

The wisest solution is self-medication. Research studies indicate that when patients control their own pain medication, they need less of it, and yet report less suffering. Recent studies of women given access to self-regulating pain-medication equipment during childbirth revealed that they used approximately half the amount of medication as did women to whom these drugs were administered. This was attributed to two factors: not only were these women able to adjust their medication instantly as needed, rather than "loading up just in case," but the fear of the pain decreased significantly once the women knew that they were in control of it. I do not doubt that a similar study among the dying would reveal the same kind of decrease in medication; the lag time between requesting drugs and receiving them has caused many dying people I've known to anticipate and overestimate their pain, since they have no means to control it themselves. In some hospitals in England, patients are given certain pain-reducing elixirs to take at their own discretion, and we would be wise to request as much autonomy as possible regarding our own pain management. It is a frightening prospect indeed to turn over control of one's own consciousness at the time of death to another human being, especially one whose philosophical values may be quite different from our own.

An equally important issue of control is whether we have a right to choose our own moment of death. Currently, we do not. If we wish to end our lives, we are forced to consult a Dr. Kevorkian, or lie to our physicians to lay away a supply of sleeping pills. These are equally unfortunate options; with no offense to Dr. Kevorkian, the controversy surrounding his work renders public what ought to be a private, self-determined affair, and puts family and loved ones in the limelight when they least need to be. Without in any way diminishing the complex ethical issues involved in the right-to-die debate, there seems to be a fundamental oversight at its center: namely, the wisdom of the dying person, and her or his ability to make conscious choices. Except in cases where people are too ill to think clearly, or have been rendered insensible by pain, it is my experience that dying people are quite dependable regarding the state of their bodies and minds, and their own wishes. To deprive them of the right to die when and how they choose is to strip them of this wisdom and render it irrelevant.

In spiritual cultures such as the Tibetan, the right to die when one chooses has never been questioned as it is in our culture. In Tibet, old lamas historically have invited people to attend the dropping of their bodies, because they are comfortable that their time has come. At the appointed hour, the lama turns around three times, sits in meditation, and stops the heart and the breath. Is this a suicide? An immoral act? Or simply knowing when the moment is ripe? It is up to the individual to decide, not the government.

We must ask ourselves frankly: is living as long as possible always the greatest wisdom? In his old age, Thomas Jefferson wrote to a fellow septuagenarian: "There is a ripeness of time for death, regarding others as well as ourselves, when it is reasonable we should drop off, and make room for another growth. When we have lived our generation out, we should not wish to encroach on another." And yet, as Sherwin Nuland has reported, it remains illegal in this country to die of old age; a disease must be noted on the death certificate.

Before I had my stroke, I was working both the telephones every morning with a forty-five-year-old man at Veterans Hospital in Los Angeles whom I had never met. He had skin cancer that had metastasized through his entire body, and one day his wife called to tell me that her husband wanted to speak to me. He described his situation; he was lying in bed, unable to move, so bloated that nurses regularly stuck a needle into his stomach to drain the fluid. Every part of his body had swollen almost beyond recognition; his testicles were so large that he could no longer sit on a toilet bowl. He said to me, "Ram Dass, am I going to make a terrible karmic error if I decide to stop this?"

What could I say? In moments like this, faced with the reality of great suffering, philosophy falls away. Could I speak to this man about evolution, the value to his Soul of hanging onto the body as long as possible? Could I take refuge in the stories of saints, such as Ramana Maharshi, who suffered stoically until throat cancer ended his life, for the sake of the devotees who loved him? This fellow had a devoted wife; I could have told him to stay for her sake, and thus avoid the responsibility of encouraging him to die. Or should I have told him to let the body go, knowing that whatever business he did not complete would be taken up in his next life? Either way, I would be interfering, and yet this fellow needed a response. I told him to go to his inner heart. I never heard what he decided.

SITTING BEDSIDE

In the 1980s, I started the Hanuman Foundation Dying Project and invited Stephen Levine to lead it. Our intention was to create a humane and spiritually supportive environment for the transformative work that death entails, and in the ensuing years, I—along with Stephen, his wife Ondrea, and later, Dale Borglum—have given hundreds of lectures, led dozens of retreats, and formed hospices and training programs for spiritual support for the dying. Such support involves a number of services, including helping people work out their final wishes, and choosing medical services. Beyond these practical functions, our primary job has been simply to hang out with people as they die and respond to what they might need.

In my early experiences with dying, I sat quietly in the

hospital rooms, appalled by the cultural pathology surrounding death. The dying individual was surrounded by lies and hypocrisy, as my Mother had been, cut off from the meaningful support of shared Awareness. I needed to do nothing more than be quiet and equanimous, and suddenly I found myself in great demand to be present at people's dying. They said that they found my presence calming and reassuring, and that I was the only person they could talk to. Family members brought me their panic, grief, confusion, anger, and pain, and all I had to do was keep my heart open and neither get caught in, nor deny, my reactions to the shifting situation.

I found that my experiences on the Soul level made my work at the bedside extremely easy. I needed to do very little, and learned early on that it wasn't my mystical pronouncements that mattered, but rather my Soul presence that served the dying. Sitting *in genuine peace* with people who were dying seemed to have a contagious effect; the spaciousness of resting in my Soul, rather than in my Ego, seemed to magnetize the consciousness of those I sat with, leading them toward silence and their own Soul's embrace. Often, I could feel this process happen; I would enter the room and find the dying person along with the people gathered around the bed, all steeped in different reactions to their own fears.

I learned to cultivate certain qualities to help in situations like these. I would try to exude non-fear. There was a woman I knew who wanted me to see her father—a psychiatrist who was in the process of dying. He was a strong personality, very hard-nosed, not a spiritual type at all. I came in as an outsider to a slightly chaotic room filled with people who were all stuck in fear. The psychiatrist couldn't really open up about his suffering, but he did let me know he was experiencing pain in his foot. I massaged his foot—and so we made contact through the body. I did this from a peaceful place, and that calmed him, which in turn calmed everyone else in the room. I was suddenly the masseur for the Soul—engaging in this small act brought everyone out of isolation and brought a little humor. When I left, everyone in the room followed me to the elevator because they had seen a major transformation in their loved one. I said I would come next week. That next week when I showed up, the psychiatrist had his sock off, waiting for his massage. What he wanted was contact with another Soul.

Elisabeth Kübler-Ross has written extensively of the experience of people dying in hospital setttings, of the stages they undergo—denial, anger, bargaining, despair, and acceptance (or resignation). Though these stages may not occur in this order, or in such precise delineation, they are generally accurate, and encountering them again and again at people's deathbeds could be challenging when I made an attempt to "fix" or teach, or to alter the circumstances in any way. Whenever I have tried to impose my model of a "good death" on a situation, or been attached to a particular outcome, it has backfired. But when I meet the person with love, without wanting anything, I become a safe haven. When I could remain conscious, aware of my own thoughts and feelings—waves of sadness or pity, aversion or fear—as well as my own temptation to react, I could bring Soul quietness, and a feeling that what was happening was all right. This inner calm seemed rocklike in its stability. I could feel people pushing against it with their own fears, testing it, but also resonating with that inner peace from a similar place inside themselves, a place behind their reactivity, a place of intuitive wisdom that each of us has behind the veil of the Ego's fears and resistance.

It was remarkable to see the openings that occurred at these deathbeds. It was as if I were waiting in the sunlight, knowing that after a while those caught in their suffering would come out of the shadows to be with me. When this happened, I could feel the cloud lifting from their psyches, and death losing its terrible onus. The sense of "wrongness" was replaced by a feeling of harmony, deepened by grief and the poignancy of physical pain. Believe it or not, I have seen desperate suffering evolve into joy in the face of death among people who thought this impossible, as they've learned to keep their hearts open and rest in a consciousness beyond the ordinary clinging mind. These transformations can seem like miracles.

Of course, not everyone who is dying will be interested, or able, to play this game, or even to consider death as a spiritual practice. I recall hanging out with Ginny Pfeifer, a dear friend and housemate of Aldous and Laura Huxley, as she lay dying of a painful form of pelvic cancer. She was a fierce humanist, and made it clear from the outset that she didn't want any of my "spiritual crap." So I simply sat by her bed, meditating with open eyes on her disintegrating body. There was deep personal pain in me because I loved Ginny and could not take away her suffering; she was actually writhing in pain on the bed. Then gradually, she and I seemed to enter a kind of stillness together. Her body continued to writhe, but the space was different. I felt as if I were bathing in bliss, and at that moment, Ginny turned to me and whispered, "I'm feeling so much peace. I wouldn't be any other place in the universe than here in this moment." I felt the same way. Such moments occur in the dying environment when the Ego of both "caregiver" and "patient" relax, making space for a less limited, less role-bound exchange to occur. When we drop these masks, the dying person is more able to move beyond his or her condition.

It is important to be aware, when sitting with people who are dying, of the subtle ways that we distance ourselves from death, and how this separation creates a trap for the person who is suffering. To protect ourselves from our own fear of death, we often set up a dynamic in which the dying person is "other," and thus hold her or him at a safe remove. When we drop such distinctions, conscious of ourselves as Souls in temporary bodies, we make way for truth to enter the room, and for the kind of bliss that Ginny and I experienced.

For many people, the aperture of consciousness narrows to the physical body when they are dying. They are so afraid, or ridden with pain, that they become preoccupied full-time with being a cancer patient, or having a bad heart or a diseased liver. Often the people attending the sick person go along with this preoccupation with symptoms, until the dying person's identity has almost ceased to matter. This is a terrible process to witness, and worse for the person whose illness has come to seem more important than their spirit. Speaking from personal experience, I've learned how important it is not to lend credibility to this reductive point of view. Often, I've had to remind myself that, just as I am not merely this paralyzed body, *I am not this stroke*, even though it has changed my life radically, and threatens sometimes to dominate my consciousness. Likewise, a dying person is not just the body you see on the bed, and the more we're able to remind them of this fact—and remember it ourselves when the time comes—the less suffering there will be. The more we affirm the many other aspects of the dying person's identity—especially their existence as a Soul—the easier it will be to maintain consciousness when circumstances conspire against it, focusing attention on the disease.

I once led a retreat on death and dying with Elisabeth Kübler-Ross. There was a large group present, and one morning a thirty-eight-year-old nurse, and mother of three, with metastatic cancer led us through an exercise. She asked us how we would feel visiting her in the hospital after one of her many surgeries, and wrote our responses on a blackboard. The list included such old standards as pity and sadness, as well as responses like, "I would be angry at God." When the list was complete, she agreed that those were, indeed, the feelings of the people who had visited her. Then she said, "You see how lonely I was? Everyone was so busy reacting to my situation that nobody was there with me."

Like any other role, being a "dying person" does not make room for the whole person, and this constriction adds a layer of suffering that only makes matters worse. A wonderful Quaker lady from Cambridge contacted me a few years back to discuss her own struggle in this regard. She was in her 60s, dying of cancer, and asked me to visit her although we had never met before. When we were alone in the room, she whispered, "Can you hurry this thing up? I'm so *bored!*"

Her comment took me by surprise; although many sick people are often bored, it is not usually their number-one complaint. I reflected a moment, then answered her. "You're probably bored because you are so busy dying all the time. Couldn't you die, say, ten minutes an hour and do something else the rest of the time?" The lady got my drift and smiled. Then we did a meditation together, in which we listened to all the sounds around us—the children playing in the yard, the clock on the mantel, the planes overhead—and felt the breezes on our faces and the softness of the light reflecting through the window. By coming into the present moment together, the drama of dying faded; suddenly, we were simply alive, two Souls resting together without roles or definition. Time seemed to stop, and when we finally spoke again, she told me that I could go. This lovely lady died peacefully a few hours later.

Death is our greatest challenge as well as our greatest spiritual opportunity. By cultivating mindfulness, we can prepare ourselves for this final passage by allowing nature, rather than the Ego, to guide us. In so doing, we become teachers to others, and our own best friends, looking beyond the body's death at the next stage in our Soul's adventure.

8

STROKE
YOGA

So here I am, some two and a half years after the stroke. The stroke gave me what I was looking for that day in February: it gave me the ending for my book. It gave me an encounter with the kind of physical suffering that often accompanies aging; it gave me a brush with death; it gave me the firsthand experiences I was lacking back then. I can write about aging now. Having the point of view of a disabled person, having come through a catastrophic physical event, I can write about aging in a way I couldn't have before.

I've always gone through experiences and then shared my wisdom about them. That's been my role. I was part of the "advance scouting party" for the psychedelic movement in the Sixties. I was part of the advance guard in the Seventies for people who were opening to Eastern religions. In the Eighties, I explored the ways we might use service as "karma yoga," as a spiritual practice—a practice that's more available to us Westerners than monastic life or other traditional methods might be. In the Nineties, as a kind of "uncle" to the baby boomers, being a little older than they are, I've been leading the way into an experience that lies ahead for most of us—the experience of aging. In the Nineties, the stroke is the learning experience which I have to share.

Of course a stroke isn't identical to aging; I didn't get any older because I had a stroke. But it is a new chapter in my aging process. The final stage of aging is cuddling up to death, and the stroke gave me some experience with that. Aging in your

60s? That's nothing. Aging in your 90s? That's a different thing. Death is much more imminent then. The stroke moved my counter forward on the board. It gave me the chance to spend some time contemplating life and death, which is usually part of the later stage of aging, when aging itself forces the issue.

The stroke was like a samurai sword, cutting apart the two halves of my life. It was a demarcation between two stages. In a way, it's been like having two incarnations in one: this is me, that was "him." Seeing it that way has been an important part of my practice, part of the way I've worked with the stroke. Seeing it that way saves me from the suffering of making comparisons, of thinking about the things I used to do but can't do anymore because of the paralysis in my hand. In the "past incarnation," I had an MG with a stick shift, I had golf clubs, I had a cello. Now I don't have any use for those things. New incarnation!

Before I had the stroke, I was full of fears about aging, and one of my major fears was about the sicknesses that might be lurking ahead. Gandhi says that before you can get to God, you've got to confront your fears. The stroke took me through one of my deep fears, and I'm here to report that "the only thing we have to fear is fear itself."

This chapter is an antidote to fear, because reading what this experience has been like for me will give you a map. It's like you're on a rafting trip, and you're about to hit some rapids. I've just been through one of those sets of rapids, and maybe my experiences can help you figure out how to handle the rapids when you encounter them.

I'm explicitly making my life a teaching, by expressing the lessons I've learned through it so it can become a map for other people. Everybody's life could be like that, if they chose to make it so; chose to reflect about what they've been through and to share it with others.

I call sickness and death "the rapids," because it's an experience of change, change, change—and change is the mantra of aging. I couldn't get a closing for this book because I had never been through an experience of fierce, dramatic change like that. I had *anticipated* what changes like that might be like, but I'd never gone through them.

Over the years, I've done practices to confront my fear of change, of which the fear of death is the foremost. In Benares, I visited the cremation grounds at the *ghats*. I sat there in meditation on the side of the Ganges, a sacred river. Bodies were being burned all around me; I smelled the burning flesh, watched the eldest son break open the father's skull with a stick to release his spirit. I'd overcome a lot of my fears about death and change through practices like that, but there still was an undercurrent of fear in my mind; I was in my 60s, I was "getting up there."

Now, having come through this stroke, I am less afraid. The stroke cleaned out some of the pockets of fear. It's happened, and here I am—closer to Maharajji than ever. What more could I ask?

The stroke happened to me for many different reasons, including karmic and spiritual ones. But on the physical level, one of the reasons for the stroke was that I had been ignoring my body. I had spent most of my life keeping my Awareness "free of my body," as I thought of it then; but I can see now that I was also ignoring my body, pushing it away. By forgetting to take my blood pressure medicine, I showed how I was disregarding my body. By ignoring the early signs that something was wrong when I was diving in the Carribean, I was disregarding my body. By over-committing myself, never saying "no" no matter what my body was telling me, I was disregarding it.

So then came the stroke.

For some days after the stroke, I was just observing. Not thinking, just observing. A friend described me during those first days as being wide-eyed, watching everything that was taking place with a kind of wonderment.

Perceptions from the outside and from the inside were sometimes very different. At one point I was in what the doctors called a "non-reactive state," and they thought I might die. From the outside, I was an object of concern and a cause for apprehension. But inside, I was just floating peacefully. My body was present, but it was irrelevant. It was like I was looking through a window, and the scene through the window had in it the hospital, and me, and the doctors, and everybody else—but I was outside looking in. I was really floating out there!

After awhile, as I started to become aware of the symptoms of the stroke, my thoughts began to come in on me. I worried for awhile about what had happened: Where had the stroke gone in my brain? How bad was it? I didn't know the answers to those questions for a long time, and that was scary. How long would the domino effect of symptoms go on? As one thing after another "went out" on me after the stroke—my knee, my hip, my shoulder, my ankle—I didn't know what would go next. How long would the pain go on—would it be days, or months, or years? I worried what the effect would be of just sitting in my wheelchair all the time, unable to move around and exercise in the usual way. That flood of questions carried strong elements of fear with it.

To work with the fear, I turned to my practices. The stroke called on all the practices I'd learned over the years: *Vipassana* meditation, *jnana* yoga, *bhakti*, *guru kripa*—at different points and in different situations I used them all. But in that particular crisis I found that I turned to Ramana Maharshi's practice of "I am not this body." I would note each part of my body, and I would say, "I am not my arm. I am not my leg. I am not my brain." That helped me avoid getting caught in the mind's fears and the body's sensations.

In the months that followed, though, I came to appreciate that, however wonderful it is as a practice, "I am not this body" is only half the truth. The stroke brought me squarely in touch with the fact that, although I am certainly *more* than my body, I also *am* my body. The stroke brought my Awareness into my body in a powerful way, with an array of physical symptoms: paralysis, aphasia, pain. The stroke "grounded" me, in both meanings of the word: it brought me in touch with the earth plane, with my body, and it made me stay at home. I used to be traveling constantly, but when you're traveling in a wheelchair, planes aren't much fun. So this illness "grounded" me, and taught me what everyone else already knew: that's it's nice to be at home.

Motels had often been my home before. I even had a story I used to tell: I was nearing the end of a sixty-city benefit tour for the Seva Foundation, and I'd been on the road for many, many weeks. In my motel room one night, I found myself thinking, "Just one more week and I'll be home!" Then I caught myself: I saw how thinking that way was a sure path to suffering—being unhappy where I was, chafing to get someplace else. So I fixed up a little *puja* on the plastic motel coffee table, with pictures of Maharajji and all. And then I took my key, walked out of the room, and closed the door behind me. I walked down to the end of the hallway, and then I turned around and walked back to my room. I unlocked the door, stepped into the room, and called out, "I'm home!"

I was trying to change my way of looking at the situation, to make "home" be wherever I was at the moment. It was a sophisticated concept—that home was the universe. And it was a useful device then, when I had to be traveling so much of the time. But my home now is an emotional haven, a center. If an animal needs to lick its wounds, it retires to its cave; it looks for a protected space. I had never known that before—that a motel room isn't a "protected space" in that way.

It's true that being "grounded" by my wheelchair has its downside. Not traveling as much deprives me of visiting the old friends I used to see in Boston, New York, all the places I used to visit on tour, and I miss that. But mostly I find that I'm very comfortable having the wheelchair. I can even see ways I cling to it. Who wouldn't rather ride than walk? Or always have a seat at parties? When I do travel, I whiz through the airport at the speed of light in my wheelchair, going "Beep-beep! Beep-beep!" to warn the pedestrians. The wheelchair is my palanquin.

Nowadays, there's a certain status in our society in being disabled. It's a political movement. I've gone to demonstrations in my wheelchair—a May Day marijuana march, and a "Dignity Day" march for the homeless, where I rolled along side-by-side with Ron Kovic (whose life was portrayed in the film *Born on the Fourth of July*). It's a new kind of role, rolling along in a wheelchair. It's made me into a different kind of symbol, because disability carries powerful symbolic values: negative ones (like *dis*-abled), but also positive ones: the blue sticker I get for parking, the accessibility issues I raise.

It's interesting the way these things work. I went to a conference at a retreat center run by conscious people who are very sensitive to accessibility problems. It turned out, though, that although I could get my wheelchair into the bathroom of the room they'd assigned me, I couldn't get it into the shower stall; the shower door wasn't wide enough. They apologized profusely, and fixed me up with a special bathtub chair—and then right after the conference, they called in an architect to begin re-designing the bathroom. That's the way it works, the way an understanding of problems spreads among people.

There are funny moments with the wheelchair. I was invited to a cocktail party one evening; it was one of those "stand-up" affairs—for everyone except me, that is. So I found that everyone else was "up there," talking to one another, and I was "down here" at chair level. Occasionally some thoughtful person would crouch down next to my chair and talk to me for awhile, and then I'd get to see a face. But for the most part, as far as I could see, the party was largely attended by a gathering of assholes.

Besides putting me in a wheelchair, the stroke gave me aphasia—a difficulty in finding the words for things. Just when the Age of Communication arrives, I get aphasia! For someone who'd made a living giving lectures and writing books, that was quite a change. I'm in the word business, and for a word merchant like me to have this particular sickness—boy, oh boy!

From the inside, the aphasia doesn't seem like a breakdown of concepts, but like an undressing of the concepts. It's as if there's a dressing room where concepts get clothed in words, and that's the part of my brain that was affected by the stroke. It took me awhile after I'd had the stroke to figure out what was going on. I had to sort out that distinction between words and concepts.

Initially, before I grasped that difference, I started to mistrust my judgment, my thinking mind (which I'd always mistrusted anyway, but on different grounds); because the concepts were divorced from the words, I could *experience* the thought-forms but I couldn't *symbolize* them. It took awhile for me to realize the difference between my thinking mind—which is clear—and my verbal ability—which is sometimes iffy.

The aphasia has introduced silences into my conversation,

and many of the people I work with use those silences to make contact with the silence within themselves. We surf the silence together, and in it they find their own answers. I've got to treat words as if they're precious now, but that's teaching me what can be conveyed with silence. When the words don't come as easily, it requires that what I say be as much "essence" as possible. I don't have the energy for all the digressions I used to run through.

I had training for this kind of thing when I was with Baba Hari Das in India. I was *mauna* (in silence) for a period of time, and he and I wrote to each other on tiny slates that we wore around our necks. When that's your way of communicating, you have to go right back to the root of things. A few words were better than many. Terse!

I've noticed something interesting: when there's not such a rush of words, the imagery gets subtler. The slower pace sometimes seems to give more poetry to my words than they used to have. I've also wondered if that's an effect of the change in balance that the stroke brought about in my brain. With the left brain—the verbal, analytical half—less dominant since the stroke, maybe the right brain is just freer to come out and play.

Besides the wheelchair and the aphasia, one other physical consequence of the stroke was the heavy encounter with pain that it precipitated. The stroke brought me into intimate contact with pain, and I found pain to be a worthy adversary for my spiritual practices. Working with constant pain pushed my practices to their limits.

I had experienced plenty of pain before—with hepatitis, kidney stones, a torn Achilles tendon. So why was this different? Partly it was the situation. In a hospital, the doctors and nurses freak out about pain, so they give you pills to get rid of it. But they don't know when to give the pills, so they ask you all the time, "Are you in pain? Are you in pain?" and that keeps focusing your attention on it. And partly it was the duration of the pain. The experiences of pain I'd had in the past were intense but relatively brief, lasting only a few days at the most. With the stroke, the pain was less severe, but it went on, naggingly, day after day, in one part of my body after another.

Pain is a potent attention-getter. A pain will call to you very strongly to be the experiencer, and you stay stuck in the experience until you can find a way to create some space around it. It took all the practices I could muster, but in the long run they worked. Practices that allowed me to jump into the Soul often worked for me—watching the pain versus experiencing the pain. I had long conversations with Maharajji about the pain. I used the practices I'd learned in my Vipassana training for making the pain the primary object of my meditation.

I still use my Vipassana techniques at night, because it's when I'm trying to sleep that I notice the pain the most—my arm, my shoulder, my foot. I can't turn over easily, or shift my position, so my muscles start to cramp up and hurt. But I have a breathing apparatus that I wear to correct a problem of sleep apnea; it magnifies the sound of my breathing, and I use that as my primary object and meditate on it until I'm in a place where I'm just quietly witnessing the pain.

One of the things I've learned in the course of all this is that I'd had some misconceptions about medical marijuana. Because I had always used marijuana (like all psychedelics) in a spiritual context, I hadn't fully appreciated its medical value. Previously I'd thought of it only for its consciousness-changing ability, but that's actually just a side effect to its use for pain relief. I live in California, a state where the use of medical marijuana is legal, and I am a "carded" patient. Marijuana has been one of the treatments that has helped me the most with the spasticity and pain I've experienced as my stroke-damaged muscles contract.

What I've learned from all this is what a delicate game it is to work with intense pain. Like all the experiences of an incarnation, pain has to be experienced fully by the Ego in order to be an effective learning experience for the Soul, but plunging in like that locks you into the pain. The only solution is to be on two planes at once: you have to enter the pain fully, and yet be in the Soul level at the same time. That's fierce! You feel the full intensity of the pain, and at the same time you transcend it by being in the Witness state. Pain demands that you establish yourself simultaneously in Ego and Soul. What an incredible teacher it is.

The stroke has given me a lot of experience with the medical world. I had no idea how many different kinds of doctors and therapists there are out there! I've learned a lot from the people who have been treating me. Dr. Zhu, my acupuncturist, has been a great teacher for me. His practice takes place in a setting which is a little unlike our usual Western clinical scene. All the patients sit together in a big waiting room, on chairs arranged along the walls. Dr. Zhu and his assistants go from patient to patient, asking questions, placing needles, making adjustments. It's all very public.

On my second visit to Dr. Zhu, I was rolled in in my wheelchair. After he had worked with some of the other patients for awhile, Dr. Zhu stepped across to the side of the room opposite me. He looked directly at me, crooked his finger, and motioned me toward him. I pointed to my wheelchair questioningly, but he gestured no. Clearly he meant for me to walk over to him. Up until then, I'd only walked with the help of a cane and the support of a therapist—but he wanted me to do it all on my own. Walk all the way across that huge room? And with all those strangers watching me besides? But I thought, "He's the doctor!" The strength of his determination got me up out of my chair, and I walked—tottering like a baby—across the room to where he stood. Therapists and doctors believe it's their *techniques* that make the difference, but I've come to realize that it's much more the power of their *certainty* that counts. It's their heart-to-heart resuscitation.

I have all kinds of therapies these days: speech therapy, occupational therapy, physical therapy, aquatherapy. All the therapies call upon me as an Ego: Try harder! Don't you want to get better? Exert your will! I've fought that; I fought it because it was pegging me as an Ego. The stroke became a playing field for a whole new level of achieving: How much "progress" has there been? Can you walk yet? More gold stars to be won. Instead of will, I've found in myself a peaceful surrender to the karmic unfolding of my life—an unfolding that's like a tree growing or a flower blooming.

Many of my doctors have been curious about me. They were curious about the fact that I wasn't reacting the way they expected me to. One doctor said to me, "How can you be happy when you've had a stroke?" I said, "Because my Awareness is on another plane." My Awareness isn't material; it's not part of the brain. Thoughts are in the brain, but Awareness isn't. That didn't seem to mean much to the doctor, but it was what was making all the difference to me.

Another doctor came into my room and said, "It's funny— I'm the head of this hospital, and where I find I most want to be is right here in this room. It's so peaceful!" It was because I was using the stroke to reflect about Awareness, and had recognized through that reflection that my Awareness doesn't have a locus, and so my consciousness isn't trapped in my body. I had *experienced* that—not as an abstract understanding, but as a real event. I was feeling the sense of peace that comes from that, and the doctor was picking it up from me.

There are people around me who trust my Awareness, and they say, "Well, *his* Awareness won't get stuck!" That's the devotion—they're the ones who assume I won't get caught, and that helps me stay un-stuck. There are other people who assume that my mind *will* be stuck, because they know theirs would be in that situation. That's most of the medical establishment—and that makes hospitals a hard environment to work in. The hospital environment identifies me with my body, and the body has been "insulted." If I buy into that, it's the root of suffering. For a long time, I've fantasized about how nice it would be if we could have a hospital that also functioned as an ashram, where patients and staff would all be satsang, and would all be doing whatever they were doing—being sick, being caregivers—as a spiritual practice. Now that I was experiencing hospital life firsthand, I *really* wished such a place existed!

Besides all the physical problems I faced with the stroke, there were some interesting psychological changes. All the roles I'd been playing, all my attitudes, were affected. The stroke took all the games I was playing, and allowed me to re-perceive them. It put my games into perspective; they seem much less important now, because I'm not so attached to the fruits they have to offer. I'm not as easily caught in wanting to be this or that for other people, to play their games. I don't feel I have to please people all the time by putting on an act for them, and so my consciousness is a little freer.

For example, I always wanted power—worldly power. That was one of the things that motivated me. For years, I was a member of organizations because they played on that desire for power, fed it in me. Now I don't find those institutions very interesting.

One of the hardest psychological hurdles I had to deal with after the stroke was the loss of independence. Getting into and out of bed. Going to the bathroom. Going someplace in the car. Preparing my meals. I need help with every one of those things. I'm embarrassed by having to ring my bell and summon my attendant for trivial things: "Would you close the window?" "Would you tie my shoes?"

Dependency has been so fierce because I used to be a super-independent person. I've always prided myself on my independence. I've come to appreciate, from my new perspective, just how much "independence" is revered in our culture, and how humbling we consider dependency. I can see the way I had absorbed those ideas from the culture, how deeply I shared them, and how much they influenced my values.

I can also see that part of the appeal of independence was not to be vulnerable. When I became dependent, I was immediately much more vulnerable. But what I discovered was that it was my vulnerability which opened me to my humanity. I saw how I had pushed away my humanity in order to embrace my divinity out of my fear of my vulnerability; and I saw the way the stroke was serving me, by opening me to that human vulnerability.

I can see now that I got my power from helping. These days, I'm helped; these days, instead of *How Can I Help?* I'd have to write a book called *How Can You Help Me?* I've gone from being the helper to being the helpee. It's a whole new role.

I see myself reflected through the minds of the people who take care of me. To one of them, I'm a job. To another, I'm a buddy. To another, I'm a sick person. To another, I'm a famous person. To another, I'm an interesting case. To another, I'm a grouch. I see the way my caregivers' personalities get reflected in their serving. Some of my caregivers hold on to an image of me as I was right after the stroke, very fragile; they're protective, they don't want me to try anything new. Others are of the "You can do it!" school and push me for all they're worth.

What I see in all our interactions is that from the Soul perspective, we're just hanging out together. Both helper and helpee are serving—they're the complementary roles in a dance. Two Souls are serving each other, honoring each other, mirroring each other's hearts. Without us helpees, what would the helpers have to do?

Since the stroke, I've found that the psychological stuff like dependency has ceased to have so much importance for me. It's not only because those things are minor in contrast with the stroke, but also—even more—because I'm more in my Soul level, where it's just, "There's independence, there's dependence, beautiful tapestry!"

That's why the stroke hasn't turned out to be as bad as I once would have anticipated—because it's pushed me up to a higher level. The "I" I am now isn't experiencing things the way the "I" I was then would have. I identify more with my Soul now, and to the Soul, things like disability and pain and dependence are just . . . poignant.

If I look at the stroke, I can interpret it at a number of different levels. There's the physical level—it was a hemorrhage in my brain. There's the karmic level—it happened because it was my karma for it to happen. And there's the bhakti level—it was given to me by my compassionate guru as a spiritual teaching. It's that last one that I find most interesting. When I ask myself, "If this is a teaching from Maharajji, what am I supposed to be learning?" I come up with a number of interesting answers.

One answer is that I've had an opportunity to practice a deeper form of karma yoga. In the Bhagavad Gita, Krishna (God) tells Arjuna (the devotee) how to use the battles of life to come to God. My stroke is one of those battles. It's hard stuff. The stroke raised the bar because it entailed so much suffering, but greater suffering elicits higher consciousness. It was Maharajji turning up the pressure for me to "get it," and it moved the game to a different league.

The stroke gave me the chance to appreciate in a much deeper way the preciousness of the love that surrounds me. The stroke created more love than I had ever seen before. Even people who don't like me sent me their good wishes! There were prayer networks, healing circles, meditation groups—I saw all these hearts opening all around me. I had tried to do that, to open hearts, through my lectures and my tapes and all, and here it was, happening all by itself. I felt love coming at me from all directions.

The love comes to me from more than just one plane, too. My shaman shows me beings of compassion on other planes. He sees them and communicates with them, and he makes me aware of all these beings who are surrounding me with love. There seems to be a whole network, reaching out with love and compassion.

I want to be part of that network of compassion which brings the multitude of beings back to the One, to love, to consciousness, to all of it. I'd like to bring myself and everyone else to that Awareness—that's always been my central purpose. The stroke took away a lot of Ego distractions, and brought me back to my Soul's purpose.

That's what healing is really all about. In the distinction that I make between healing and curing, healing is what brings us closer to God. Curing means bringing you back to what you were—but if "what you were" wasn't closer to God, then you haven't been healed. I haven't been cured of my stroke, but I have definitely been *healed by it*. Healing moves us closer to the One, and if you're the One then you're whole. That's the ultimate in healing—"making whole"—because there's no longer anything left out, including the sickness.

When people ask about me, they often say, "Is he all right?" That always makes me think of a story about Maharajji. He was surrounded by a group of people, and he said, "Somebody's coming." They said, "Nobody's coming, Maharajji." "Yes, yes, somebody's coming." Just then a man entered the ashram— the servant of one of Maharajji's old devotees. Maharajji looked at the man and said, "I know—your master had a heart attack, but I'm not coming."

"He's been calling for you, Maharajji," the servant said, "and he's been your devotee for so many years."

"No, no, I'm not going to go," Maharajji said. Then he picked up a banana and handed it to the servant and said, "Here. Give him this. He'll be all right." Now in India, when the guru gives you a piece of fruit, it's like the wish-bestowing tree; anything you want happens. So the servant rushed home with the banana. They quickly mashed it up and fed it to the man. And as he took the last bite, he died.

So what's "all right"? We at least have to consider the possibility that dying at that moment was the most "all right" thing that could have happened to that man—that Maharajji's banana opened him to his death, and brought him closer to God. That's healing, not curing.

Because the stroke brought me all these teachings from Maharajji, brought me into my Soul level, I call it grace. But it's not the "easy" grace I'd known from Maharajji in the past. It took me right to that edge between Maharajji's love and the ferocity of the stroke, so I call it "fierce grace."

In the time right after the stroke, as I started to assess what it had done to my body, to my plans, to my expectations, I felt a flash of anger at Maharajji. It reminded me of an experience I'd had with my stepmother, Phyllis, some years before. Phyllis was a wonderful, feisty woman, and I'd come to love her a lot. She had developed cancer, and the question was whether it had metastasized to her liver, which would be fatal. They had done a biopsy, and they were going to call with the results.

Phyllis had asked me to be on the phone with her. I was in

the bedroom, sitting on the floor, doing some writing, and the phone rang. I picked up my phone and Phyllis picked up hers and the nurse on the other end said, "Just a minute—the doctor is coming." I looked up at a picture of my guru, and I said to Maharajji, "Look—I don't ask you for anything, because you know how things are, and how things have to be, so what am I asking for? But if you could just slip it through, karmically, without any trouble, would you . . ." At that moment, the doctor came on the line and said, "Mrs. Alpert, I'm sorry to tell you this, but the cells in your body show the worst kind of malignancy. The cancer has spread. You only have about six months to live."

I felt my heart close, and freeze; and I looked at the picture of Maharajji and I said, "You son of a bitch!" It shocked the hell out of me—I mean, I *never* spoke to him like that! But I was *furious*! And then a moment later, I felt a flood of love filling my heart. I realized I was meeting Shiva, I was meeting change personified, and I said, "Yeah, that too!" And I was that much closer to Maharajji. We had just cut through, he and I, another level of that kind of "goody-goody" part of the devotion trip, and had moved into a place where we were recognizing each other across the universe, with *all* of its chaos and *all* of its horror and *all* of its change.

The same thing happened with the stroke. There was a surge of anger—the feeling, "How could you let this happen to me?!" And then as I turned on Maharajji with all my fury, I felt his love just pouring into me, and I felt closer to him than ever. I was learning the lessons of fierce grace.

At that point I realized that I had been dealing with a very "refined" sort of grace in the past—the loving kind of grace, the grace of the good things that kept happening to me. "Fierce grace" means I've now been given a fully rounded understanding of grace. Now I have a full view of what grace is all about.

But it's like learning to love Shiva or Kali—two deities who represent destruction and ferocity. It's learning to love *whatever* it is that brings me closer to God.

We suffer because of a desire, an attachment, a clinging, so our suffering points the way to where the work is. With suffering, there's suddenly a lot of motivation to rid yourself of the desire, and not much motivation to hang on to it—and the more desires I let go of, the freer I become. So as Maharajji would say, "See? That's the way it works. Suffering does bring you closer to God."

What was changed through the stroke was my attachment to the Ego. The stroke was unbearable to the Ego, and so it pushed me into the Soul level also, because when you "bear the unbearable," something within you dies. My identity flipped over and I said, "So that's who I am—I'm a Soul!" I ended up where looking at the world from the Soul level is my ordinary, everyday state—not an occasional experience, with psychedelics or for some other reason, but my everyday reality. And that's grace. That's almost the definition of grace. And so that's why, although from the Ego's perspective the stroke is not much fun, from the Soul's perspective it's been a great learning opportunity.

There's a paradox here, because although I'm more in the spirit now, I'm also more human. Before, I was always protecting myself from the desires of the Ego. To a renunciate, the material world represented temptation, so I was busy pushing it away. Now I can risk going deeper into my incarnation, because I'm feeling more secure in my identity with the Soul. When you're secure in the Soul, what's to fear? There is no fear of death, of anything your incarnation can bring. And it's interesting the way it works in both directions, because the very fact of entering my incarnation more fully than ever brings me more fully into my Soul.

I'm taking more risk with my consciousness these days. I can let the kite-string out a lot farther. It's scary sometimes; it's like going into outer space, and you're afraid of getting lost out there. Sometimes I'll find my consciousness someplace and I'll ask myself, "Now how did I get here?" I let myself get farther away from home plate than ever.

More and more, I'm becoming an appreciator of silence. For many years I have been attracted to the teachings of Ramana Maharshi, who gave most of his teachings without ever saying a word. He would sit in silence, and the people who sat with him would come away with the answers to their questions. Just a couple of months before my stroke, I had narrated a video about Ramana Maharshi. The video was released during the time I was at the rehab center, and two of my friends brought a copy of it to the hospital for me to see. At one point in the narration, I heard myself saying, "Ramana Maharshi usually taught in silence." Watching that moment, there in my post-stroke state, I smiled and nodded. "In silence". . . I understood that place much better now.

I speak fewer words outside these days, and I also have fewer words inside. My mind is much quieter than it used to be. Instead of an urge to be busy all the time, I'm happiest just sitting at home, watching the trees, watching the clouds, watching the birds. I don't need to schedule every minute—birds don't have schedules, why should I?

I'm much closer to Maharajji than I've ever been. I spend much more time hanging out with him every day than I used to. The stroke brought me closer to Maharajji because it brought me closer to my center—the hot center, the life-and-death issues. I have been able to open to this stroke, to go along willingly on the journey, because I saw that it was another unfolding of Maharajji's plan.

My link to Maharajji is very strong. He's the very context

of my existence. He's my friend, my constant imaginary play-mate. He's an imaginary playmate who's wise, loving, under-standing, rascally—all the things I like in a playmate. What's wonderful is that that kind of playmate is available to each of us, because it's inside.

The guru is the ambassador of Awareness. The guru helps us unite the Soul with Awareness, with God by helping us con-nect with the part of ourselves that is already divine. Guru Kripa is the path to this union. In this practice, we begin seeing the events of our lives as acts of grace—because each event is an opportunity for practicing devotion. It's a method of trust, of seeing Maharajji as showing compassion toward me. It's a method of the heart, of how much I love him. And his kripa, his grace—fierce or otherwise—is his love back to me. It's a heart-to-heart connection.

Guru kripa is a form of bhakti, of devotion, in which love is at the root of the faith. Love God, love guru, love your own inner being—any of them will take you through, and eventually will show you that they're all the same thing. In the *Ramayana*, Hanuman says to Ram—to God—"When I don't know who I am, I serve you; when I know who I am, I am you." That's the Soul's destination in the journey—to become that statement.

The Soul wants only God. Because the Soul's single mo-tive is merging with God, it doesn't value its own individuality. The Ego clings desperately to identity—the Soul is trying to get clear of individuality in order to merge into the One.

The stroke was Maharajji's lightning bolt to jolt me into a new place in my consciousness. The ferocity of the method tested my faith, but in the end my faith held. My bond with Maharajji was strong enough to withstand the doubts. His love and his presence were strong enough to outweigh everything else.

Maharajji is what opened my heart to that kind of love

and faith. He's just my "special example" of faith—yours is whatever it is for you that represents God or Spirit or that larger screen of things.

My relation with Maharajji is one of faith: that what comes to me from him is grace. If I have faith in that, then there is no place in my life, no event in my life, where that grace isn't, and all the suffering of the stroke is just the honing of my faith.

This book is more of my "advance scout" role. These days I'm the advance scout for the experiences of aging, and I've come back from the scouting party to bring good news. The good news is that the spirit is more powerful than the vicissitudes of aging. My stroke was a good test for my faith; the bar was high. I came away from the stroke firm in my faith, and I know now that my faith is unshakeable. That assurance is the highest gift I have received from the stroke, and I can say to you now, with an assurance I couldn't have felt before, that faith and love are stronger than any changes, stronger than aging, and, I am very sure, stronger than death.

EPILOGUE:
THERE
WE ARE

As my father grew older, he slowed down a lot, as people often do. He began to approach each task with great deliberation and patience; each action, whether getting into the car, climbing the few steps to the house, or settling into his favorite armchair, was accompanied by such attention that it became almost a kind of meditation. He found satisfaction in the completion of each small task; he would smile with contentment and say quietly, "There we are."

You and I have been exploring together, through the vehicle of this book: trying to figure out what this next stage of our lives might be like, and how it might fit into the deeper dimensions of our being. My wish for each of us is that we might settle into aging with that feeling I sensed in Dad, that feeling of release and completion and fulfillment . . .

. . . There we are!

CREDITS AND PERMISSIONS

At Eighty-two: A Journal by May Sarton. Copyright ©1966 by the Estate of May Sarton. Used by permission of W. W. Norton & Company, Inc.

Choices in Healing: Integrating the Best of Conventional and Complementary Approaches to Cancer by Michael Lerner. Copyright ©1994 Michael Lerner. Used by permission of MIT Press.

Quote written by Nadine Stair. From *If I Had My Life to Live Over I Would Pick More Daisies* by Sandra Martz (editor). Copyright ©1992 Papier Mache Press. Reprinted by permission of Papier Mache Press.

Selected Poems, published by Bloodaxe Books Ltd. Copyright © Jenny Joseph 1992.

"Prolong not the past. . . ." From *The Snow Lion's Turquoise Mane: Wisdom Tales from Tibet* by Lama Surya Das. Copyright ©1992 Lama Surya Das. Used by permission of Harper San Francisco.

Song Celestial or Bhagavad-Gita (1885), translated by Edwin Arnold. Kessinger Publishing Company, 1942.

How Proust Can Change Your Life: Not a Novel by Alain de Boton. Pantheon Books, New York, 1997.

For information about Ram Dass's teaching schedule,
or a catalog of his audiotapes and books, write to:

Ram Dass Tape Library
524 San Anselmo Ave. #203
San Anselmo, CA 94960
or call (800) 248-1008
or check the Web site at *www.RamDassTapes.org*

ABOUT THE AUTHOR

Ram Dass, who in the 1960s left his teaching position at Harvard to blaze a new spiritual trail, shaped the awakening consciousness of a generation with his landmark two-million-copy bestseller, *Be Here Now.* A cofounder of the Hanuman and Seva foundations, he works with environmental organizations, the socially conscious business community, and the dying. He lectures around the country and lives in northern California.